12th October 1105.

To   Daddy

From Catherine.
with Love xoxoxoxox

THE COUNTY DONEGAL
RAILWAYS

OTHER DAVID & CHARLES RAILWAY HISTORIES

OTHER DAVID & CHARLES BOOKS ON NARROW GAUGE RAILWAYS

OTHER DAVID & CHARLES BOOKS ON IRISH RAILWAYS

THE
COUNTY DONEGAL
RAILWAYS

by

EDWARD M. PATTERSON
DSc, MRIA, FRSE

DAVID & CHARLES
NEWTON ABBOT   LONDON   NORTH POMFRET (VT)

First published 1962
Second edition 1969
Third edition 1982

British Library Cataloguing in Publication Data

Patterson, Edward M.
  The County Donegal railways.
  1. Railways, narrow-gauge—Ireland—Donegal (County)
  I. Title
  385'.5'0941693   HE3049.D/

  ISBN 0–7153–8167–9

Printed in Great Britain
by Redwood Burn Ltd, Trowbridge Wilts
for David & Charles (Publishers) Limited
Brunel House Newton Abbot Devon

Published in the United States of America
by David & Charles Inc
North Pomfret Vermont 05053 USA

Contents

            Lists of locomotives, railcars and trailers, and coaching
            stock are printed on folding sheet inside back cover.

Illustrations

IN TEXT

CHAPTER I

The Coming of the Railways

THE COUNTY AND ITS PEOPLE

Donegal in the north-west of Ireland is a county of strong scenic contrasts. Its magnificent coastline varies from towering cliffs pounded by the Atlantic waves, to quiet sheltered bays and shell-sand beaches, protected from the storms by rocky islands. Inland, the country is wild and rugged, but the great mountains of quartzite and granite fall to glens and pastoral lowlands. In the eastern part of the county, farmland stretches between Lough Swilly and the valley of the River Finn.

The river valleys of Donegal lie along two well-defined directions, the most obvious from north-east to south-west. This direction is represented by the remarkably straight Gweebarra and Owencarrow Rivers and by the Barnesmore Gap, and it is followed for shorter distances by many other small rivers. Linking these main valleys are others, less well defined, which run from west-north-west to east-south-east. The middle part of the course of the River Finn is determined by one of these. The valleys intersect the mountains and the transport routes naturally developed along them.

Set against this physical background, the population was steadily increasing in the early years of the 19th century. Donegal's maximum was recorded at the 1841 Census, when 296,000 people were resident in the county. Before the next decennial census was taken, the whole of Ireland had suffered the tragedy of the Potato Famine. For three successive years the staple crop of the people was affected by blight and failed to yield. There were no chemical fungicides then and many of the populace had to choose between emigration or starvation. County Donegal suffered heavily. In 1851 it held 41,000 people fewer than a decade earlier. In 1861 the figure was down by a further 18,000. From then until the end of the 19th century emigration led away an annual average of 1,600 people from County Donegal and a tradition had become established which has persisted up to the present time. The 1966 Census showed that the population of 108,000 is now only 36 per cent of what it was 125 years ago. This corresponds to only 56 persons to the square mile. Apart from the three urban towns of Buncrana, Bundoran and Letterkenny, which had populations of 2,916, 1,421 and 4,522 in 1966, there are only six towns of over 1,000 persons. These are, the twin towns of Ballybofey/Stranorlar (1,942), Ballyshannon (2,223), Carndonagh (1,058), Donegal town (1,507), Killybegs (2,062) and Moville (1,061). The present pattern of population is widely dispersed, but concentrations occur in the fertile valleys, in the lowland area around Donegal Bay and around the intricate coastline. Apart from the urban settlements listed above, the rest of the people live in a dozen or so small villages or in the very numerous farms. By cross-channel standards, the farms are tiny and in the county as a whole 57 per cent of the farmers work less than 30 acres of land. Indeed in the Glenties rural district nearly one-third of the farms have areas of less than five acres.

To appreciate how the Donegal Railways system came about one must first look at the railway that preceded it, and to which the Finn Valley Railway, precursor of the County Donegal Railways Joint Committee, was originally joined.

THE LONDONDERRY—ENNISKILLEN LINE

Construction of a railway southwards from the city of Londonderry, or Derry, as it is locally called, began in 1845 under the ægis of the Londonderry & Enniskillen Railway Company. Its line followed for much of its course the obvious route along the major river valley. For 12 miles south from Derry the broad valley of the River Foyle led the line to the market town of Strabane. Here the Foyle gave way to the confluence of the Rivers Finn and Mourne, the former coming in from the Donegal highlands to the west. The Londonderry & Enniskillen ran up the valley of the Mourne to Newtownstewart, where the river changed its name to the Strule, and continued alongside the river to Omagh.

The L & E was built piecemeal, as were many other lines at that time. From Derry, Strabane was reached in 1847, but the income from those 12 miles of railway was not up to expectations. Competition came from the neighbouring canal that allowed access from the River Foyle to a canal basin in the town of Strabane. It was not until 1850 that money and drive were available to carry the line further towards the south. Newtownstewart and Omagh were reached in 1852. Thereafter, climbing speedily, the line came to a summit near the market town of Fintona and then dropped towards its terminus in Enniskillen, where it arrived during 1854.

Omagh became a junction in September 1861, when the Portadown, Dungannon & Omagh Railway, worked by the Ulster Railway Company, came in from the east and linked the L & E's line to Belfast. Down at Enniskillen, the Dundalk & Enniskillen Railway had connected Lough Erne with the east coast since 1859.

Though the Londonderry & Enniskillen had the benefit of no less a person than Robert Stephenson in the planning of their course, they made a poor enough show of running their railway. Not only was the permanent way difficult to maintain, but the locomotives were underpowered. The company became financially embarrassed and by 1859, only five years after completing the line, asked their southern neighbour, the Dundalk & Enniskillen, to undertake the operation of their line. So the D & E leased the L & E

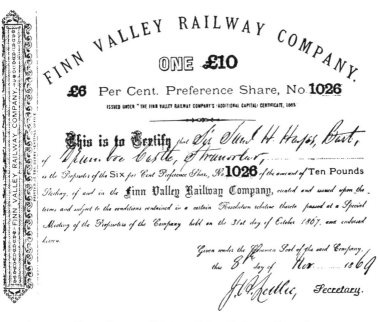

Share Certificate for one £10 Finn Valley Railway Share, issued on 8 November 1869 to Sir Samuel H. Hayes, Bart, of Drumboe Castle, Stranorlar, and signed by J. A. Ledlie. The FVR Company's seal is impressed in the lower left corner of the certificate, but is not seen in the print

from 1 January 1860. Thereafter, the L & E were content to be absentee landlords, holding their meetings in London, and drawing an annual rent. Paying a steady if unexciting dividend, the L & E remained as a separate company until absorption into the Great Northern Railway of Ireland in 1883.

CHAPTER II

The Finn Valley & West Donegal Railways

STRABANE TO STRANORLAR

As we have seen, Strabane stands at the point where the Rivers Finn and Mourne join and flow seaward as the Foyle. The town is on the east bank, and is in County Tyrone; on the west is the much smaller village of Lifford, which is in County Donegal. The River Finn forms the boundary between the two counties there, and for some miles upstream. Strabane had a railway from 1847, and a service both to Derry and to Belfast from 1861.

Fourteen miles above Strabane, the twin towns of Stranorlar and Ballybofey straddled the River Finn. The two largest landowners in the neighbourhood, the 4th Viscount Lifford and Sir Samuel Hayes, Bart., were naturally anxious that the benefits of a railway should be brought from Strabane into their own part of the country. At their instigation preliminary surveys were made in 1859 to establish the course of a line of railway between Strabane and Stranorlar. The Finn Valley Railway Company was registered. Towards the preliminary expenses, Lord Lifford and Edward Hunter of Blackheath, London, lent £4,000. On 15 May 1860 Royal Assent was given to the Finn Valley Railway Act and authority was obtained for the issue of £60,000 of share capital, and for borrowing powers of £20,000.

The first meeting of the newly-constituted Board of Directors was held in London on 22 May 1860, when there were present Lord Lifford, Sir Samuel Hayes, Alexander R. Stewart, of Ards, Donegal, and Dr Robert Collum of Hyde Park Square, London.

A series of meetings were held through the month of June. Sir Edwin Hayes, Bart., was appointed interim secretary, a post which he held until his death in the following month. Then, on 21 July, a Mr Murphy was appointed secretary at a salary of £100 per annum. Murphy did not remain in office for more than a few weeks; the Minutes say nothing of the way of his going, but he was succeeded by James Alexander Ledlie, who was to stay with the railway until 1890. In the summer of 1860, the Board appointed John Bower as resident engineer, and Peter Barlow, F.R.S., as engineer-in-chief.

At an early date, Bower was instructed to inspect the 'double-headed longitudinal rail' on the North London's line at Bow Station, and to prepare specifications using 'the Yankee or flat-bottomed rail' and 'Adams's Patent double-headed rail'.

The prospectus of the Company contained details of a census of road traffic that had been taken between 10 and 16 July in the Finn Valley between Stranorlar and Strabane, though it was not stated exactly where. During the period surveyed the observers were passed by:

Vans	12
Carts	909
Jaunting Cars	275
Gigs	14
Horses	106
Passengers conveyed in the above vehicles	2308
Passengers on foot	1105

It was noted that 'this is a week when the farmers were working at the harvest, and there was therefore not a great deal of agricultural produce being moved'.

The first call on the proprietors, of £2 per share, was made on 6 July.

A canal, four miles in length and with two locks, had been built between 1791 and 1796 by the Marquis of Abercorn to link Strabane with the navigable part of the River Foyle towards Derry. From 1 July 1860 it was leased to the Strabane Steam Navigation Company Ltd, sometimes called the Strabane Steamboat Co. On 6 August 1860, the Finn Valley Board authorised their chairman, Lord Lifford, to write to Major Humphreys of the Steamboat Company, to enquire whether that concern would be interested in taking shares in the Finn Valley Railway Company. But with a net annual revenue of around £300, the steamboat people were quite unable to participate. Neither were they able to offer the railway company any promise of reopening the River Finn for navigation. Some decades before, small steamers had been able to reach Castlefinn, while the Foyle was used for the regular delivery of coal to Lifford.

At the Board Meeting of the FVR on 11 October, the secretary was instructed to write to six well-known contractors inviting tenders for the construction of the line. Letters were sent to Messrs. McCormick, Rose, Hartland, William Dargan and the partners Greene and King. The position was reported to the proprietors at their first Ordinary Meeting, held in Simm's Hotel, Strabane, on 29 October 1860. The encouraging report of the engineer-in-chief was read:

> 26, Great George-Street, Westminster.
> October 23, 1860.
>
> My Lord and Gentlemen
>
> Having in compliance with your instructions recently examined the line of your railway with Mr. Bower, I have the satisfaction to be able to report, that by the adjustment of the gradients, and some deviations in the line, reductions in the earthwork from the Parliamentary section, to the extent or nearly of quite one half may be made, and that the character of the material of which the cuttings are composed is extremely favourable, as appears from the trial holes recently excavated. I may remark, that in my extensive experience in railway construction, I have not met an instance where the facilities for executing a railway are more thoroughly combined: the earthwork is favourable and inconsiderable in quantity; the bridges few in number; the ballast is every where at hand, the roads are convenient for taking the material to the work, and the rails and sleepers being obtained on favourable terms, I have no hesitation in stating that the Finn Valley Railway may be executed for a less sum than has yet been expended on any railway in the United Kingdom, and can also, from the gradients being favourable, be worked at a cheap rate. I have the honour to be, my lord and gentlemen,
>
> Your obedient servant,
>
> PETER W. BARLOW.

By the time of this meeting, contracts for the rails and fastenings had been effected. It had been decided to use orthodox permanent way and to lay it as 65-lb. flat-bottom rails fixed to transverse sleepers. Experience in such matters had broadened during the previous 20 years, in Ireland as elsewhere. The near neighbours, the L & E, were already regretting their adventures in untried permanent way. As the proprietors were told:

> Investigation as to the weight of the rails suitable to your line, and enquiry as to Adam's permanent way, occupied your Directors for many days in London, and resulted in the adoption of the 65 lb. rail, the fishplates etc. which you will see described in your Engineer's plans and specifications. Adam's permanent way being a recent invention, your Directors did not venture to adopt it on so small a line as yours.

The contract for the permanent way was made with the London firm of Messrs Levick & Co., who were to supply:

> 'rails of the best quality at the rate of £6 5s; fishplates at £9; bolts and nuts at £16; screw bolts at £13 per ton delivered in Derry— £2,000 of the payment to be taken in shares. . . .'

The directors reckoned that they had secured a bargain with these prices, and went further in making for the cheapest sleepers they could get. They bought 25,000 of them, split from native larch into half-rounds and costing half-a-crown each.

At the second half-yearly meeting at Stranorlar on 27 April 1861, the chairman reported that repeated surveys were being made 'to ensure the best line'. Since the valley floor is flat and subject to periodic flooding in places, it was important to locate the line between marshland on the one hand, and the firm rising ground that flanked it on the other. The choice lay between heavy bottoming over the waterlogged ground and the higher cost of land and of excavations along the sides of the valley.

The River Finn flows from west to east between Stranorlar and the small village of Clady, and there the railway was kept to the north of the river. Below Clady the river turns north-east towards Strabane. Near Urney House, one mile from Clady village, it was proposed to cross the line to the south-east bank of the river so as more conveniently to make a junction with the L & E's line. From the river crossing at Urney the three-mile stretch lay in County Tyrone.

By the end of the winter of 1861, shipment of the rails and fastenings from Levick & Co. was imminent. They were to come to Derry, and there to be transhipped to Strabane. Still anxious to curtail expenses, Ledlie wrote to Dawson of the Londonderry & Enniskillen Railway on 31 January 1861:

> 600 tons of rails are now due for shipment to Derry. What rate per ton wd. you charge from Derry to Strabane, including loading and unloading and storage of the rails till required? The Canal Company sent their lighter from Derry to Castlefinn, when they got to learn of the rails coming and offer low terms and free storage. . . .

On 30 March Messrs Levick wrote to say that they had chartered no less than six small ships to bring over the rails. They had the *Joseph* with 230 tons, *Kate* 210 tons, *Samuel Roper* 185 tons, *Countess of Morley* 170 tons, *Furnessbuss* 155 tons and *Hope* 135 tons. It must have been quite an armada that came up the Foyle in early April, and still the Finn Valley had not chosen their contractor! But they at least had 1,085 tons of rails stacked ready for laying. Payment for them was making Ledlie uneasy and on 1 April 1861 he had written to Lord Lifford to tell him that '*All* the Balance to our credit in the Bank wd. not pay for 1,085 tons and we wd. be without any money to buy land'.

It was time to encourage the shareholders. They were presented

Page 17: BUSY TIMES AT DONEGAL TOWN

(above) Orange Demonstration special, 12 July 1906. Old carriage shed on right, later removed; (right) The road is made for the last train out of Donegal, on 31 December 1959. On the left Signalman Willie Hegarty, on right Stationmaster Willie Johnston; (below) Railcars for Strabane and Killybegs, and from Ballyshannon (Nos. 20, 19, 18), 20 August 1959

Page 18: STATION SCENES—1

*(above) No. 2 with Orange Demonstration special, Bruckless, July 1958;
(centre) No. 4 and two container flats at Castlefin, August 1958; (below)
No. 2 on Letterkenny goods, 1950, at Strabane*

with a rosy picture of the estimated costs and income.

Expenditure:

Parliamentary and Engineering expenses		£3,412
Land		£8,000
Sleepers		£3,200
Permanent Way, partly laid		£8,500
Contractor's Work		£20,000
Total		£43,112

(Equivalent to £3,080 per -mile)

Income:

Estimated at around £12 per mile per week, giving a total of £8,112 per year.

Presenting these facts, Lord Lifford enthusiastically promised the shareholders a dividend as high as 11 per cent.

None of the six contractors approached in the previous October had managed to secure the contract. The work was re-advertised on 20 March 1861, tenders were to be in by 18 April, and this time the work was given to Messrs Moore Bros. As later events showed the decision was not a wise one, for completion of the civil engineering work took far longer than had been forecast, while the estimate was greatly exceeded.

The question of termini next exercised the Finn Valley Board. At Strabane the obvious choice was already there, owned by the Londonderry & Enniskillen and since January 1861 in the charge of the Dundalk & Enniskillen. Not only was it proposed to share the station at Strabane, but to enter it over 30 chains of the L & E main line and avoid having to build a separate bridge across the River Mourne. To the FVR Board it seemed reasonable to carry these arrangements a stage further and to get the D & E to supply motive power, carriages and wagons, and to work their line for them. For this service the Finn Valley were to pay the Dundalk & Enniskillen 35 per cent of their gross receipts.

Their Stranorlar terminus was to house their administrative headquarters, and it seemed proper to the Finn Valley Board that the building should be commensurate with their prospects. Plans for a station and offices, to cost around £1,500, were advertised for competition. Of 24 entries, that of Mr Clayton of Bristol was judged to be the best and was awarded a prize of £25.

At the end of the summer of 1861 came the ceremony of formally turning the first sod. The site chosen was in a field a short distance from the intended junction with the L & E's line, in the townland of Castletown, County of Tyrone, about half a mile from Strabane.

Contemporary reports of the ceremony on 9 September 1861 describe a scene that must have lived long in the memories of the Finn Valley folk.

> Flags and streamers were hoisted, the Royal Ensign occupying the most conspicuous place. The brass band of the Prince of Wales' Own Donegal Militia were present under the leadership of Bandmaster Griggs and enhanced the proceedings by the performance of several pieces of choice music.

Amidst this gay setting, near the slow-flowing Finn, the vice-chairman, James Thompson Macky, J.P., rose to address the guest, Lord Abercorn, and requested him to raise the first sod. 'His Lordship, amidst the applause of the assembled spectators, divested himself of his coat and wheeled away the turf on a highly-ornamented barrow, specially prepared for the occasion'. Lord Abercorn spoke to the gathering and having prophesied a most successful future for the undertaking, called for three cheers for the Finn Valley Railway. The cheers were echoed by three more for Lord Abercorn who, his duty accomplished, returned at once to Baronscourt ten miles off 'owing to the serious indisposition of a relative of his lordship's'. To wind up the proceedings in a suitable manner, 'at 2 o'clock the Directors entertained a select party in the spacious dining room of Simm's Hotel, Strabane'. The railway had been launched and the contractors promised completion within nine months.

At the fourth half-yearly meeting on 29 April 1862, John Bower's report dispelled some of the rosy haze of optimism. The progress made by the contractors over the winter had been disappointing. Incensed by the delay and the loss of the expected summer traffic, Mr Maude, a director, criticised Bower's report as being vague, and called for more specific details. It then emerged that only between a quarter and a third of the excavations had been finished, though the contractors had 'recently hastened' and had at the time between 600 and 650 men at work. Nothing had been done between Strabane and Castlefinn. In support of the contractors, Mr Lewis claimed that much of the delay was not of their making, but was because they had not been given the land at the time specified. In spite of this, the chairman, Lord Lifford, hinted strongly that the penalty clause of £100 per week might be invoked if work was not speeded.

The intake of share capital was still much below the authorised

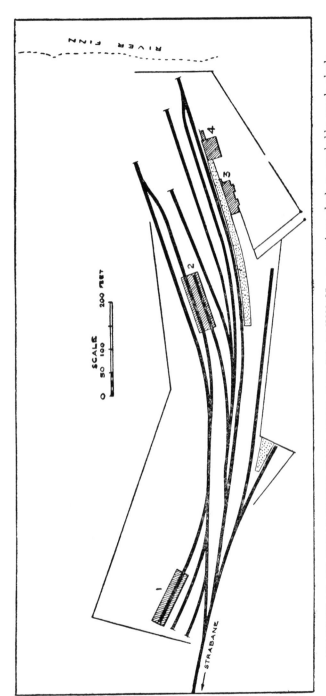

STRANORLAR IN BROAD-GAUGE DAYS (FINN VALLEY RAILWAY). **1**, carriage shed; **2**, probably goods shed; **3**, station and offices; **4**, store

amount, and to complete the works it became necessary to turn elsewhere for ready cash. An extraordinary general meeting was held in the hotel at Stranorlar on 20 May 1862, and authority was given by the shareholders to borrow £20,000 from the Public Works Loan Commissioners. This was obtained at 5 per cent interest, the principal to be paid back in 18 annual instalments beginning in October 1865.

By October 1862 the line was still far from complete. The directors had not yet invoked the penalty, but they had been faced with the unpalatable information that the line was going to cost considerably more to build than had been forecast. A figure of around £60,000 was mentioned. They had no choice but to continue.

Gathered at the sixth half-yearly meeting at 11 a.m. on 18 April 1863 in the now familiar surroundings of Simm's Hotel, Strabane, the proprietors were given reports from their directors and engineer which showed that, at last, their line was nearly complete. The rails were laid throughout. All the stone bridges and culverts were finished to the copings. The stations were ready for roofing and, except at Stranorlar, the signals had been erected. The Urney Bridge near Clady was only partly completed, but the superstructure, a pair of continuous lattice girders each 222 ft long, was being erected. The chairman, Lord Lifford, encouraged the audience with the news that he, in company with J. A. Ledlie, Robert Russell, a director, and John Bower, had come up the line in 38 minutes that very morning on board an Irish North Western engine. Nine months previously, the D & E, proud that they were working not only their own but also the L & E's line, had obtained Parliamentary sanction to change their title to Irish North Western Railway.

It took the whole of the summer of 1863 to finish the work. By then, relations between the Finn Valley Board and the contractors were distinctly strained, each party finding fault with the actions of the other. Apparently the contractors were short of ready cash, for the Board Minutes mention that a sum of £706 0s 4d for labourers' wages was to be debited to Messrs Moore Bros. Or more likely, the Company had decided to finish some parts of the work themselves and charge the contractors for it. The cost of construction was now able to be determined and at the proprietors' meeting in October it was admitted that the bill was almost £70,000, or £5,300 per mile.

Much sobered, the Company at last saw their line complete. They informed the Board of Trade, and Captain Rich inspected the line during August. He wrote his report in Stranorlar on the 18th of the.

month and, though generally satisfied, expressed slight doubts about the rails. The line was:

> laid with the flat bottomed or contractor's rail, in lengths of 18 to 25 feet, and weighing 65 lb per lineal yard. It is fished, and fixed to transverse sleepers, with fang bolts at the joints and dog spikes in the intermediate sleepers. The rail is only 4½ in. in the bottom flange and the line should not be worked at great speed. ...the ballast is of sand and gravel laid about 1 ft. thick.

Captain Rich's statement tells us that turntables were erected at 'the Junction and at Stranorlar' while 'a passenger platform was ordered to be erected forthwith at the Junction'. By 'Junction' he no doubt meant Strabane station, rather than at the actual divergence of the FV and INW lines.

Board of Trade sanction to open was given on 20 August. The Lord Lieutenant of Ireland, Earl Carlisle, officially declared the line open for traffic on 7 September 1863, almost two years to the day since the ceremonial turning of the first sod. Promise of high dividends had faded, it remained to be seen how nearly the traffic receipts would correspond to the forecasts.

From the start, three classes of passengers were carried. Up to the end of 1863, representing 16 weeks of operation, the traffic receipts were:

Passengers.	1st class	771	...	...	...	£87	5	8
	2nd ,,	1,635	...	...	...	£116	6	3
	3rd ,,	12,498	...	...	...	£479	9	7
Excess fares		...	...	...	...	£5	14	5
Goods and livestock			...	...	...	£395	0	9
Parcels, horses, carriages, dogs				...	...	£28	4	0
Total	...	...	...	...	...	£1112	0	8

This scale of receipts, less than half what had been expected, though admittedly in autumn and wintertime, cast further gloom on the management. It was obvious that once the Irish North Western Company had taken their percentage, there would be insufficient to pay any dividend on ordinary shares.

Applications for shares continued to be disappointing, and by the end of 1863, interest payments were in arrears on the £20,000 loan. The Company still owed money to the contractors and to others totalling almost £13,000. Revenue had to be used to pay bills that should have been covered by capital. The dark picture was unrelieved by the gross income figures for the whole of 1864, the first complete year's working, which totalled only £3,441.

Steps were taken to augment the inadequate capital and the Finn Valley Railway Co. (Additional Capital) Certificate 1865 authorised the issue of £20,000 of 6 per cent preference shares. The proprietors were reluctant to commit themselves to the entire burden of interest on these at first, in spite of the still-enthusiastic words of their chairman, and they only sanctioned the restricted issue of £6,000. By the end of 1867 only £2,120 of these had been taken up. During 1865, the interest on the Government loan was reduced to $3\frac{1}{2}$ per cent, and four years later arrangements were made whereby the Company repaid both interest and capital at the rate of £1,300 per year, so that the debt would be extinguished by 1887. With all these efforts, it was not until 1869 that the Capital Account cleared its feet. In the first half of that year an ordinary dividend of $1\frac{1}{4}$ per cent was declared for the first time.

During these years of inadequate finances, the Minute Books contain many references to the iniquities of the INW. It is clear that the Finn Valley were in a cleft stick, for in saving themselves the expense of making their own station at Strabane, they had become committed to sharing it with the Irish North Western and entering it over 30 chains of Irish North Western line from Finn Valley Junction. For this privilege their hosts at Strabane exacted an annual rent of £375, and showed no inclination to reduce it. While the sum may have seemed fair in those far-off days of 1861, eight years of fact-facing had made the Finn Valley think otherwise.

By the time of their 21st half-yearly meeting, the Finn Valley seem to have been driven nearly frantic by the position. A dividend of 2 per cent was declared by the chairman, and Lord Lifford went on to say that 'the original agreement was with the L & E' and that 'we never expected to fall into the hands of what was then called the D & E'. He demanded that the Company obtain 'absolute . . . independence of the Irish North Western Company'. The rent of £375 was paraphrased as equal to 2s 2d per train mile for the three trains that ran each way over those 30 chains of the main line every day. The real or imagined iniquities of the INW were catalogued: 'they ask us to supply all permanent way materials, to pay for flood damage, and to make all enlargements at stations which they, not us, think necessary'. It is obvious that the original agreement left something to be desired, and that the Irish North Western, secure in their practical experience, were not prepared to risk their stock on a badly-maintained line. The Finn Valley were paying for their early innocence.

Criticism was made, too, of the INW's traffic management. It was claimed that passengers on through journeys were being subjected to long delays at Strabane, the Finn Valley trains being unpunctual, 'especially the 4.5 p.m. arrival at Stranorlar'. The Irish North Western was criticised as well, for failing to keep the telegraph in working order.

In an effort to short-circuit their tormentors, the Finn Valley seriously considered making an independent line into Strabane. They employed an English consultant to survey such a scheme, and a map was prepared to accompany the application to Parliament. The new line was to diverge one furlong before the existing junction, and to run parallel to the INW line, crossing the River Mourne by a separate bridge. Strabane station was to be by-passed and from a point north-west of it the line was to swing out towards the river bank and back, rising above the INW line on a sustained curve of 10-chains radius and coming to a terminus close to the Strabane Canal, a quarter-mile nearer to the centre of the town than the INW station. A short spur, of 1½ furlongs, linked the start of the curve with the INW line. Needless to say, the Irish North Western opposed the bill in the 1871 Session, and it failed to pass the House of Lords. The Earl of Erne was blamed for this and was subjected to caustic criticism at the next half-yearly meeting, it being pointed out that he held £100,000 of shares in the INW, but only £1,200 in the FVR.

By the end of 1871, release from bondage was in sight and had the Finn Valley been strong enough financially, and able to take advantage of the end of their ten-year agreement with the INW, they might have continued to struggle for independence. But they were aware that they were still comparatively inexperienced in railway operation. So they went half-way. They decided to buy their own carriages and wagons, to maintain their own permanent way, to staff their own stations, and to leave the Irish North Western to look after the motive power at a cost of 9d per mile. The fixed charge for the use of Strabane station rankled, but was unavoidable.

So in April 1872, the Finn Valley contracted with Messrs Brown, Marshalls & Co. of Birmingham for the supply of two tri-composite carriages, one third-class carriage, two third brakes, one horsebox, one carriage truck, and four open and 23 covered wagons. They congratulated themselves on the purchase, for shortly afterwards prices rose appreciably. The new agreement with the INW came into effect from 1 November 1872, and although their engines continued to steam into Stranorlar yard, at least the Finn Valley could see

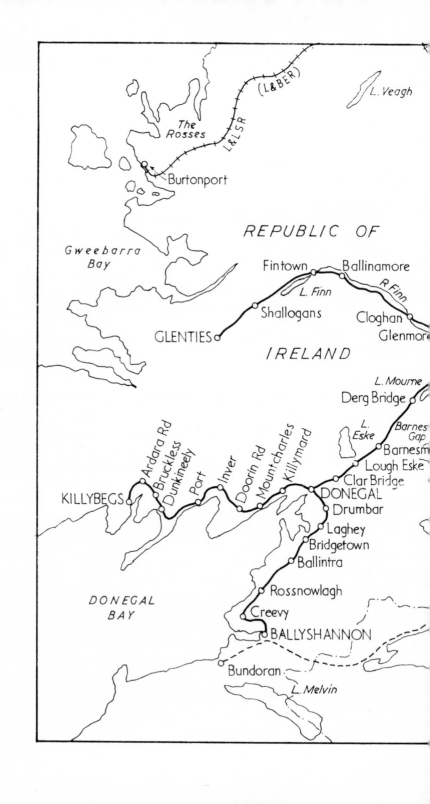

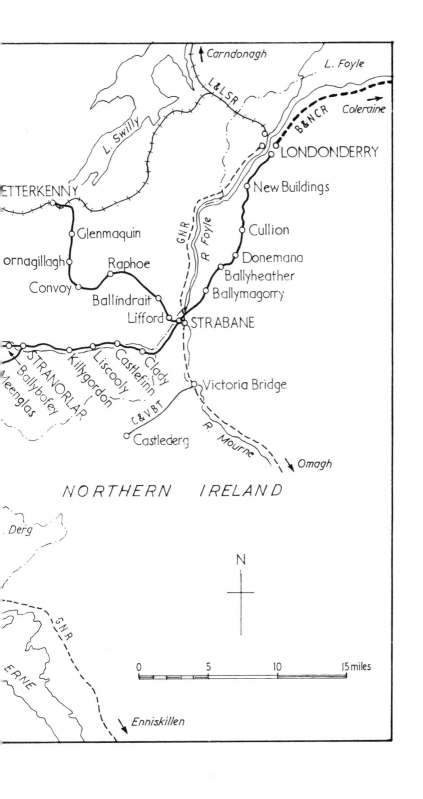

↑ Carndonagh

L. Foyle

L&LSR

B&NCR — Coleraine

LONDONDERRY

L. Swilly

LETTERKENNY

New Buildings

GNR

R Foyle

Cullion

Glenmaquin

Donemana

ornagillagh

Raphoe

Ballyheather

Convoy

Ballymagorry

Ballindrait

Lifford

STRABANE

STRANORLAR

Ballybofey

Meenglas

Killygordon

Liscooly

Castlefinn

Clady

Victoria Bridge

C&VBT

Castlederg

R. Mourne

↘ Omagh

NORTHERN   IRELAND

. Derg

N

GNR

ERNE

0   5   10   15 miles

↓ Enniskillen

their own initials on the sides of the carriage and wagon stock.

By the time of the half-yearly meeting in April 1873, the new rolling stock had received an airing and Joseph Kerrigan, a Stranorlar shareholder, spoke approvingly: 'Our comfortable, handsome carriages are a great boon, especially when one remembers the rickety, leaky old things that were supplied by the Irish North Western Company'.

Kerrigan had figured at the proprietors' meetings before, when he had maintained that the Finn Valley's future lay, not in terminating at Stranorlar, but in Donegal town. In that he had the support of Lord Lifford, but the latter was quick to emphasise that such a project had not been supported by the townspeople of Donegal. It is likely that their reluctance arose from the fact that since 1866 Donegal town has only been 11 miles as the crow flies from the line of the Enniskillen, Bundoran & Sligo Railway. That railway line could have been reached across easy country, while by contrast the Finn Valley terminus lay 18 miles away, behind the barrier of the Blue Stack Mountains.

The traffic returns of the FVR showed a steady increase throughout the 1870s, both in passenger and freight takings. By 1878 the dividend was up to 2½ per cent, a poor enough figure when compared to the forecasts, but it did seem that at last more prosperous times were approaching. In 1876, the INW had amalgamated with other lines to form the Great Northern of Ireland, and under them the old arrangements at Strabane were continuing.

THE WEST DONEGAL LINE

In 1878, Kerrigan's repeated pleas for a Donegal extension were answered, albeit in a modified form. Experience was being gained 50 miles to the east in the iron-ore mining plateau of Co. Antrim in the use of the novel gauge of 3 ft, and the Finn Valley Board were not slow to notice this pioneering work.

Rather than involve the Finn Valley Company in the venture of a Stranorlar—Donegal extension, a separate company was formed and on 21 July 1879 the West Donegal Railway Co. was granted powers to build a 3-ft-gauge line between the two towns. Of their capital of £150,000 one-third was in loans.

The Board of the WDR was under the familiar chairmanship of Lord Lifford; James Musgrave of Belfast was deputy chairman. For their seal they chose the arms of the Conyngham family, impaling those of Derry, with 'Tyrconnell' for the motto.

The course of the West Donegal line was largely determined by the topography, and it was found that the Barnesmore Gap offered the only feasible route through the Blue Stack Mountains. In the absence of any considerable village *en route*, the most direct way was indicated. Only near Stranorlar did the line diverge far from the road; it swung sharply to the south to cross the River Finn, and thence turned westwards, climbing steadily past Lough Mourne to a summit near Derg Bridge, a lonely stream-crossing at the eastern end of the Barnesmore Gap.

The first ordinary general meeting of the West Donegal Railway Company was held on 15 January 1880 in the Corporation Hall, Derry, and J. A. Ledlie was appointed secretary at a salary of £150 per year. He continued to hold a similar position in the Finn Valley Company, and the station buildings at Stranorlar served as joint headquarters.

No time was lost in putting the West Donegal work out to contract, and on 20 April 1880 the directors met to consider three tenders. Having regard to the physical difficulties of the route the contract prices were remarkably similar to each other: £33,805 from Collen Bros., £32,223 from Messrs McCrea & McFarland, and £32,261 from Thomas S. Dixon. Dixon was persuaded to reduce his quotation to £31,000 and to accept £5,000 of that in the form of ordinary shares, and was awarded the contract.

On the following day the Earl of Mountcharles, son of the Marquis of Conyngham, who owned much of the land to be traversed, took a spade and ceremonially turned the first sod. Among those present to witness this first move in the direction of Donegal were Viscount Lifford, Sir Samuel Hercules Hayes of Drumboe, James Barton, C.E., and fittingly, the vociferous Stranorlar proponent, Joseph Kerrigan. The gathering then adjourned to lunch as the guests of Lord Lifford, driving up to the house of Meenglas, set high on its hillside to the south of the line.

The summer of 1880 passed without any further civil engineering work, and the serious business of finding money for the job was undertaken. On 17 June an extraordinary meeting of West Donegal proprietors authorised the Company to borrow up to the limit of £50,000.

Dixon began work on 1 August 1880 and by the end of the year he was employing 800 labourers. The exceptionally severe weather caused almost complete suspension of work for seven weeks as snowstorms swept the bare moorland leading up to the Gap. Best Baltic redwood instead of local larch was specified for sleepering.

Once again, Lord Lifford's enthusiasm was to be tempered by the chill of shortage of money, for which he repeatedly blamed the lack of support from the town of Donegal. By the spring of 1881 it was clear that there would not be enough capital to complete the line to Donegal town. It was fortunate that Dixon had not started work from there, or the railway would not have reached Stranorlar where its workshops and sheds were. As it was, the disappointed Board decided to form a temporary terminus beside the main road in the townland of Druminin, clear of the Gap, a short way from the picturesque Lough Eske and four miles from Donegal. The unavoidable was deplored, but it was hoped that a large traffic in red Barnesmore granite would develop.

In August 1881, James Barton, as engineer to the undertaking, reported to the proprietors at the half-yearly meeting, held in the Stranorlar terminus:

> . . . your works have made fair progress. The portion of your line under contract is nearly formed throughout from Stranorlar to a temporary terminus at Druminin. Out of the contract quantity of 168,000 cubic yards of earthwork, 154,000 have been excavated. Out of fourteen bridges, eleven have been built, two are in progress and one is to build. One hundred and ten culverts have been completed and seven remain to build. Seven and a half miles of permanent way have been laid, and the rails, sleepers and fastenings for the remainder have nearly all been delivered . . . the plans for the station works have been matured, and at Stranorlar arranged with the Finn Valley Railway Company, and a contract has been entered into for a goods store and engine and carriage sheds at Stranorlar, which are in progress. The remainder of the station works, signals etc. can now be commenced immediately. I fear the contractor will be hardly finished at the contract time in October, but he will not I think be much behind.

By this time, a roadside tramway from Portrush to Bushmills, in County Antrim, was in course of construction and it was planned to work it by hydro-electric power. This pioneering spirit appealed to one of the West Donegal shareholders, James Corscadden, who was a director of the Londonderry & Lough Swilly Railway. Corscadden suggested at the meeting that the West Donegal should complete their line to Donegal as an electric tramway. While hydro-electric power could undoubtedly have been generated locally, the proposal was too novel to appeal to the majority, and it was not followed up.

Although the Finn Valley were nominally a separate company and were not directly responsible for making the West Donegal line, they were intimately involved in the latter's finances, to which they agreed to contribute £2,000 per year. The drain on the Finn Valley's

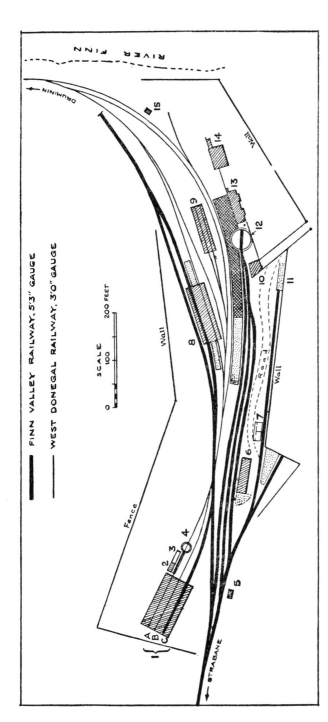

STRANORLAR IN MIXED GAUGE DAYS (FVR AND WDR). **1A**, WDR engine shed; **1B**, WDR carriage shed; **1C**, FVR carriage shed; **2**, WDR water tank; **3**, WDR coal store; **4**, WDR turntable; **5**, FVR East signal cabin; **6**, FVR goods store; **7**, FVR cattle pens; **8**, tranship shed; **9**, WDR carriage shed; **10**, FVR coal store; **11**, FVR carriage dock; **12**, FVR turntable (45') and water column; **13**, station and offices; **14**, store; **15**, WDR West signal cabin

slender financial resources was to be offset by the income of 70 per cent of the West Donegal's traffic receipts. This arrangement showed undue faith in the future of the West Donegal. In effect the Finn Valley lost by the deal.

The Finn Valley further agreed on 15 March 1881 to work the West Donegal line, and to control that Company's rolling stock. Since 1878, James Larrissy had been the Finn Valley's superintendent of carrying stock, but left before he could add the West Donegal vehicles to his care, and for a few months in 1882 was succeeded by J. W. Barber. As Barber followed Larrissy from the service, the post was abolished, to be replaced by that of locomotive superintendent, with D. Laverty as the first holder.

Three 2—4—0T locomotives had been ordered from Sharp, Stewart & Co. at a cost of £1,195 each. Barton reported to the Board on 27 February 1882 that not only had they been delivered, but that one of them had been tested on the ascent to Barnesmore Gap with a train of 110 tons.

Anxious to pay tribute to their chairman, the West Donegal Board named the three engines after three of Lord Lifford's relatives, and *Alice*, *Blanche* and *Lydia*, as sturdy brass nameplates, were duly attached to the side tanks.

The coaching stock of the West Donegal consisted of three tricompos, five third-class carriages, three brake-thirds, two carriage trucks, and a horse box. The goods stock consisted of 40 covered wagons, three open wagons and two brake vans. Accommodation for all had to be made at Stranorlar, and from being a quiet Great Northern road-end, the yard assumed a more complex appearance with broad-gauge track leading in from the east and narrow-gauge leading out of the west. The engine and carriage shed had three roads, two narrow-gauge for the engines and carriages, and one for the Finn Valley carriages. The West Donegal had a small turntable on the road in to their engine shed; that for the Finn Valley was then at the west end of the station, where the Glenties branch later diverged, though a larger broad-gauge turntable was later built immediately east of the station. No photographs taken during the mixed-gauge days at Stranorlar are known to exist, but fortunately manuscript plans have survived.

The Board of Trade inspection was made by Major General Hutchinson, and his 7½ manuscript pages of report, dated 11 April, give valuable detail of the new line. Land had been taken for a double line, but the works were for a single line only. The only sidings were at Stranorlar and though there were no public stations

Letter, dated 10 September 1890, from R. H. Livesey to J. D. Nott, Esq. of Donegal. 'Yours of yesterday. I will leave here tomorrow by 12.25 pm train for Lough Eske, for the purpose of going over the Light Railway with your Directors & Mr. Barton, prior to its being taken over from the Contractors.' (The Light Railway which is referred to is the Druminin to Donegal extension) on the 14 miles of line, a platform had been provided in Carrick-magrath townland for the use of Lord Lifford. (It was later named Meenglas Halt.)

The rails were 27 ft in length and weighed 45 lb to the yard. Sleepers were of Baltic redwood, 6 ft long and 8 in x 4 in in cross section. They were set at 22 in centres at the rail joints, and at 30 in centres elsewhere. The only sharp curves were of 6 and 7 chains on leaving Stranorlar, both had check rails. Chief engineering works were the Finn viaduct and three masonry underbridges. The river viaduct had four spans of 40½ ft and four of 12 ft. There were neither tunnels nor level crossings over public roads.

Stranorlar had the only turntable. One had not been installed at Druminin, engines had to work back bunker first, and because of this the General recommended that speeds should not exceed 25 miles per hour. There was no block telegraph, and the line was to be worked with only one engine in steam or two coupled together. The General concluded:

> In consequence of the steep gradients, the line will require most careful working and I should strongly recommend a break van or break carriage being placed at each end of each train. Where the line passes through the Pass of Barnesmore a careful watch will be required to see that no large boulders coming from the hillside endanger the safety of the traffic.

On 25 April 1882, the West Donegal Railway was opened between Stranorlar and Druminin. There appear to have been no inter-mediate stations, and the train service consisted of three trains each way, a journey time of 40 minutes. Horse-drawn cars brought passengers the last four miles into Donegal at a charge of 6d.

Before long the narrow-gauge trains discovered that in their traverse of the wild Donegal hills they would have to match their forces against more than the gradients. The Barnesmore Gap formed an enormous natural funnel for the westerly gales that from time to time swept in from the Atlantic. Through the confines of the Gap and beyond it, there could sweep down towards the Finn Valley winds of hurricane strength. On the night of 12 December 1883, Sam Bingham was driving a special of engine, carriage and van up the bank from Stranorlar when, to quote his own words, he 'was brought completely to a stand by a head wind near Meenglas'. That incident was but a foretaste of what was to happen six weeks later, when the wagon, carriage and brake van of the 5.55 p.m. Stranorlar—Druminin train were lifted bodily off the rails by a side wind, an occurrence described more fully in Chapter 19.

Page 35 : STATION SCENES—2

(above) Unloading sugar, Bruckless, 20 August 1959; (below) Railcar No. 18
at Ballintra, 20 August 1959

Page 36: WITH THE GOODS

*(above) No. 6 arriving at Lough Eske, July 1955, from Stranorlar;
(centre) No. 2 leaving Letterkenny, August 1952; (below) No. 11 on
goods from Donegal, passing West Cabin at Stranorlar, August 1952*

JOINT WORKING

On their own section of line, the Finn Valley Company had found that their early decision to use local material in the form of half-round larch logs had been false economy. After less than ten years some were rotten, and in August 1872 it was reported that the Irish North Western were replacing them with new larch timbers. The Board asked the INW to use 'creosoted foreign wood' and agreed to pay the difference in price. A larch sleeper cost 2s 6d, the imported sleepers 3s to 3s 3d.

By 1882, now looking after their own permanent way, the Finn Valley were systematically replacing any old sleepers still left with rectangular creosoted Baltic redwood, and relaying with steel rails in place of iron.

For the next six years the Great Northern continued to work the Finn Valley Company's line, while the Finn Valley worked the West Donegal's line. The arrangement with the Great Northern seemed to work well enough and the Finn Valley were content not to have to face the expense of purchasing their own engines.

Financially, the link-up between the West Donegal and the Finn Valley was proving a severe drain on the limited resources of the latter. The termination of the narrow-gauge line at Druminin was both disappointing and embarrassing and Lord Lifford made energetic efforts to raise the necessary capital to close the four-mile gap. The West Donegal Light Railway Order (1886) was the outcome, authorising £19,000 of share capital to be issued. Work was started by John Hegarty of Larne, Patrick Diver of Donegal building the gate houses, but Lord Lifford did not live to see the scheme completed. He died in 1888, and his place as chairman on the two boards was taken by his son-in-law Sir Samuel Hercules Hayes.

The country between Druminin and Donegal was very different from the wild mountain scenery through which the line had come. Typically lowland, it sloped gently downwards through a country of small farmsteads, first through hummocky gravel moraines and then across rounded clay drumlins reminiscent of much of County Down. There were no major engineering works, but a good deal of excavation and filling were needed to bring the line to grade.

The finances of the extension were inadequate to deal with the construction of a station at Donegal, and a separate company was formed to attend to that necessary matter. The Donegal Railway Station Company first met on 10 August 1888 in Simm's Hotel,

Strabane. Their capital was £2,500. The tender of £745 13s 1d from John Hegarty of Larne for earthworks, and of £1,633 18s 8d from Sam Hepburn for the erection of the station were accepted. The station was rented to the West Donegal Company on completion, at £200 per annum in perpetuity.

Work on the extension went slowly; it was inspected by Major-General Hutchinson on 9 September 1889 and was opened on 16 September.

Widespread poverty and the continuing decline in the population of Ireland, legacies from the Famine years, had focussed the attention of the British Government on the need for assistance to raise the general standard of living. The assistance took various forms, capital investment in improved transport being considered one way of benefitting the people.

GOVERNMENT LINES

In 1888, the Royal Commission on Irish Public Works made suggestions for the development of the railway system by means of light railways. The Light Railways (Ireland) Act of 1889 followed, and enabled promoters to apply for state aid towards the cost of further or new construction. The profits, after all outgoings had been met, were to be divided equally between the promoters and the State. Two Orders were made under this Act, and provided for extensions both to the FVR and the WDR. The first to be passed was the West Donegal Light Railway (Killybegs) Order 1890, and covered the building of 19 miles of 3-ft-gauge line from Donegal to Killybegs. In the following year the Finn Valley (Stranorlar and Glenties) Order authorised a similar injection of money: a nominal £1,000 of baronially guaranteed stock and an interest-free Government grant of £123,886. Together these financed 24 miles of 3-ft-gauge track to the head of the River Finn and down the Shallogan River valley to the small town of Glenties. The dreams of Lord Lifford were to be realised at last, though he had not lived to witness their fulfilment.

The contract for the Killybegs extension was let to Thomas I. Dixon. For the work he bought a new 0—4—0ST engine (Hunslet No. 564) and named it *Bruckless*. It was offered for sale in January 1894 and was later used on various English and Scottish works.

The Glenties contract was obtained by the Londonderry firm of McCrea & McFarland. They had close connections with the Board of the Londonderry & Lough Swilly Railway, through Mr John (later Sir John) McFarland, and it was not surprising that an engine from the Swilly line came to be used for the ballasting. It was No. 1 of the L & LS stock, an 0—6—2T built in 1882 by Hawthorn & Co., and named *J. T. Macky* after the Swilly's first chairman.

In August 1890, J. A. Ledlie resigned from the secretaryship of the Finn Valley after thirty years' service. An annuity of £100, equal to a third of his salary, was granted to him and he was co-opted as a director. These moves created violent opposition from a small section of the Board. A critical circular had been sent to all the shareholders by two English Board members, Mr Hunter and Dr Collum, commenting adversely on Ledlie's work and character and recommending that the annuity be withheld. As a result the half-yearly meeting on 19 August was a stormy one. A detailed reply was given by Sir Samuel Hayes, the chairman, both on the subject of the Company's finances and on the vexed question of Ledlie's annuity. Ledlie's place was taken by R. H. Livesey, who had been with the North Wales Narrow Gauge Railways Company and whose experience enabled him also to take on the duties of locomotive superintendent, replacing Laverty.

The fact that the Glenties line was to be narrow gauge pointed to the next move. It had become clear to the Finn Valley Board that the hinterland of their line could not yield anything like the traffic originally forecast, and it was unlikely to increase significantly. The Finn Valley had paid no dividend to their shareholders since 1879, due largely to their unfortunate West Donegal commitments. Losses had to be cut, and on 27 June 1892 Parliamentary sanction was given to the amalgamation of the Finn Valley and the West Donegal companies, creating the Donegal Railway Company.

CHAPTER III

The Donegal Railway

RATIONALISATION AND REGAUGING

The rationalisation was to proceed further. Broadening experience of the 3-ft-gauge lines was being obtained in County Antrim, and indicated that this narrow gauge was well suited to districts such as Co. Donegal. In the north of that county, the neighbouring Londonderry & Lough Swilly Railway had regauged their line in 1885. The Finn Valley decided to follow suit, for by converting their own line to 3-ft gauge they would be enabled to cast free from their attachment to the Great Northern.

Early in 1891 the Finn Valley asked James Barton, as consulting engineer, to give his opinion on the suggested change of gauge. On 5 March 1891 he wrote from Dundalk to R. H. Livesey, enquiring whether new rails would be needed, and if the sleepers were in a good enough state to permit a groove to be formed in them and one rail let in to the new gauge.

The entry of their proposed narrow-gauge line into Strabane gave the new Donegal Railway Company food for thought. To avoid further payment of station rent to the Great Northern, they would have to build their own station, yet to facilitate interchange of traffic the two stations must be adjacent. To share the Great Northern's bridge across the River Mourne, between Finn Valley Junction and Strabane station, would have required mixed-gauge track. The DR decided to be quite independent in this matter, to abandon the old FVR junction and enter Strabane over their own bridge, parallel to and a short way west of the Great Northern line. The 1870 scheme was thus resurrected in a modified form.

In 1893, powers were obtained for the Company to build six furlongs of new railway, and to alter the gauge of the whole Finn Valley section, or to lay a third rail and have mixed gauge. The Great Northern, seeing a small if steady income coming to an end, unsuccessfully lodged a formal objection.

Work on the changes began soon afterwards. In October 1893,

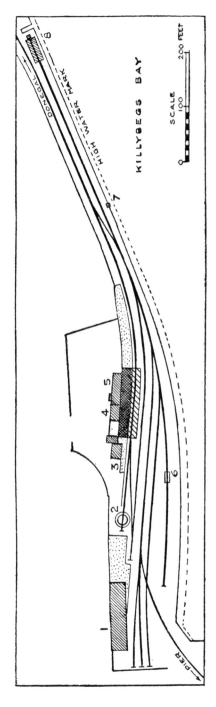

KILLYBEGS. **1**, goods store; **2**, turntable (31′); **3**, water tank; **4**, agent's house; **5**, station; **6**, weighbridge; **7**, signal cabin (later removed); **8**, engine shed (later removed)

the contract for the new Mourne Bridge was awarded to Edward Manisty of Dundalk at £2,450, and in December, Edward Radcliff reported that the contractors were making satisfactory progress. Three-quarters of the earthworks and masonry were complete, as were the bridge foundations. The iron superstructure was ready for erection. The contract for the station buildings had been let to Campbell & Son of Belfast and the foundations had been put in. Radcliff reckoned that if all went well the line would be completed by May 1894. On 5 April, Livesey gave the Great Northern formal notice of his Company's intention to cease to use Strabane station in the near future.

The work was not quite finished in time for the 1894 summer, but narrow-gauge track had been laid up to the broad gauge by July. The stage was set for the change-over. This was done in one week-end. Between the night of Friday 13 July and Sunday 15 July, construction gangs toiled all along the Finn Valley section, bringing in the rail furthest from the platform as Barton had suggested and respiking it to the undisturbed sleepers. There was no need to resort to mixed gauge, nor to lay two parallel lines of different gauge for a time as the Ulster Railway had done when they shrank their gauge from 6 ft 2 in. to 5 ft 3 in. in 1846. On Monday 16 July the Finn Valley section was reopened on the narrow gauge.

Some months later the Board of Trade got around to inspecting the alterations, sending across Major Marindin to look them over. On 2 April 1895, the Major's report was sent from the Board of Trade to Livesey. Though in general his opinion was favourable, Major Marindin made certain recommendations. At Clady, the platform needed to be lowered, and a second stretcher rod fixed at the points. He mentioned incidentally that the layout at Castlefinn consisted of a single platform and a siding, and he considered that the platform needed similar lowering to that at Clady. Between Liscooly and Killygordon his eagle eye detected two deficient fish-plates. At Stranorlar, the waiting room on the down platform required to be completed, and various signalling changes were called for at both the East and West signal cabins.

Already on 18 August 1893 the Donegal—Killybegs line had been opened. With a narrow-gauge mileage then of 37, the Company required more engines and rolling stock, and six 4—6—0 tank engines were delivered by Neilsons, while the carriage stock was augmented by 17 vehicles. All of the new carriages were bogie type, and included six composites, five third-class and six brake third-class. The wagon stock also received considerable additions.

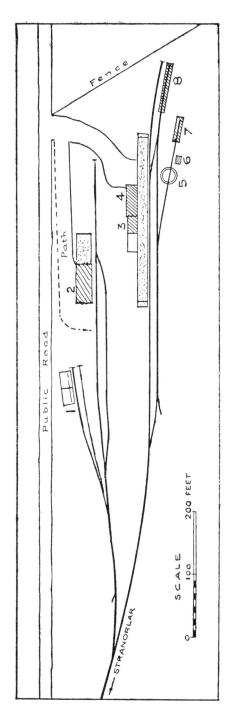

GLENTIES. **1**, cattle pens; **2**, goods store; **3**, agent's house; **4**, station; **5**, turntable; **6**, water tank; **7**, engine shed; **8**, carriage shed

The broad-gauge Finn Valley rolling stock had been rendered redundant by the regauging. After only 22 years it was in comparatively good condition and capable of many years of useful work. The Great Northern must have hauled it away, but was not interested in buying second-hand stock, since its new Dundalk shops were fully capable of building anything needed. So it went to the far side of Dublin, being bought by the Dublin, Wicklow & Wexford Railway for £1,000.

Construction of the Glenties branch was proceeding. It diverged from the West Donegal line at the western end of Stranorlar station. A curved platform extension was made for it up to the limits of the river bank. The River Finn was crossed by a girder bridge, a massive affair laid a stone's throw downstream from the road bridge connecting the twin towns of Stranorlar and Ballybofey. The line ran through sparsely-populated country. Traffic began on 3 June 1895, and after half-a-year's working that Board regarded the receipts as 'entirely satisfactory'.

The mileage of the Donegal's system was now 75 and under the new management income was steadily increasing. Emboldened, the Board were taking steps to promote bills for further extensions, one to Derry and the other to Ballyshannon.

GOVERNMENT HELP

On 14 August 1896, the Railways (Ireland) Act was passed. It offered particularly generous terms where a proposed line passed through what was now officially termed a 'Congested District'. Such districts were, in Ireland, comparatively thickly populated but with farm holdings of insufficient size and quality to give economic support to their owners. Donegal qualified as a 'Congested District' and the Company became keenly interested in the likelihood of further branches being added to their system at Government expense. Some hint of what might have been built can be gathered from a coloured map, drawn by James Barton in 1896 and circulated at the time. The northern and north-western part of the county was still without railways and the Company were evidently anxious that any developments should connect with them, and not with their potential competitor, the Londonderry & Lough Swilly Railway. This concern, originally co-eval with the Finn Valley and like it a broad-gauge line to begin with, now owned 13 miles of 3-ft-gauge track linking Derry and Buncrana. They also worked the 16½-mile Letterkenny Railway which, at Burt, made an end-on

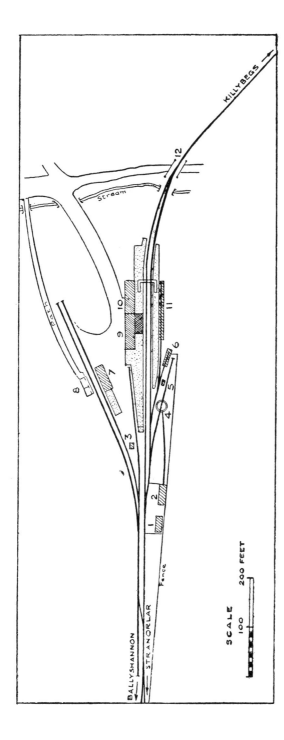

DONEGAL. **1**, permanent way shops; **2**, permanent way store; **3**, signal cabin; **4**, turntable (30'); **5**, water tank; **6**, engine shed; **7**, goods store; **8**, cattle pens; **9**, station; **10**, agent's house; **11**, carriage shed; **12**, level crossing junction with their own line. Letterkenny was a prosperous town by Donegal standards and was an obvious jumping-off place for northward extensions.

Barton's 1896 map, drawn on a scale of four miles to one inch and measuring 30 in. by 22 in., shows four 'probable Government Railways', none of which was built as shown. The most important of the four is shown boldly connecting Strabane with Letterkenny and, once into the L & LS territory, continuing northward to Ramelton, Milford and Carrigart before turning westward to Creeslough and Dunfanaghy. The length would have been about 50 miles.

The second branch would have served the north-west of the county. Leaving Fintown, it crossed the watershed between the Shallogan and Gweebarra River valleys and headed into the rock-strewn district of The Rosses to end, somewhat indecisively, midway between Bunbeg and Gweedore. For some reason it ignored Burtonport, with its fishery pier.

The third line was a simple extension of the Glenties branch, four miles in length, to the village of Maas and peculiar in that it did not continue for another three miles to the pier at Narin. Finally, a westerly extension of the Killybegs branch was shown, out to the coastal villages of Kilcar and Teelin, where there was a 'government' pier.

Two years after the publication of Barton's map, an Order was made under the 1896 Act which sponsored a modification of the first two 'probable Government Railways'. Much modified it was, not only in its course but also in its management, and it was the 49¾-mile Letterkenny & Burtonport Extension Railway. Opened in 1903, it was handed to the L & LS to work. Although the Donegal Railway had hoped to benefit from the 1896 Act, they were to be disappointed. Only the Strabane—Letterkenny link came to be built, a part only of the projected Strabane—Dunfanaghy branch; as we shall see it came much later, for practical purposes a part of the Donegal's system, but built largely as the result of private enterprise and at a time when Government support for such projects had long ceased.

Had the Killybegs-Teelin extension been constructed, it would have been a spectacular one, reaching into some of Donegal's wildest scenery and ending near the mighty sea cliffs of Slieve League, which rise 2,000 ft above the Atlantic. It would justifiably have rivalled the Valentia branch, and the Mallaig extension of the West Highland Railway.

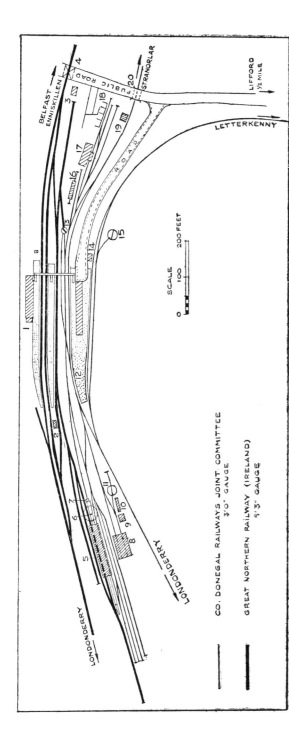

STRABANE. **1**, GNRI passenger station; **2**, GNRI North signal cabin; **3**, cottage; **4**, GNRI level crossing; **5**, tranship shed; **6**, crane; **7**, hut; **8**, CDRJC engine shed; **9**, water tank; **10**, hut (formerly Coach 37); **11**, turntable; **12**, CDRJC passenger station; **13**, tranship turntable (13); **14**, signal cabin; **15**, railcar turntable; **16**, coaling stage (chassis of Coach 55); **17**, goods store; **18**, cattle pens; **19**, water tank; **20**, masonry overbridge.

EXCURSIONS AND REFRESHMENTS

At Stranorlar, R. H. Livesey was fulfilling his duties most efficiently and in November 1896 his salary was brought up to £600 per annum. Under his managership the activities of the line broadened. Realising now that they need not expect heavy passenger traffic to materialise from their hinterland, the Company took steps to encourage excursion traffic from outside the system. In May 1897 the Board decided to rescind a previous resolution against the running of excursions on Sundays and Livesey (now general manager) was given authority to arrange these provided that the number of persons taking part was kept below 300.

The provision of some form of refreshment for travellers was considered. Strabane was an obvious place for a refreshment room. Private enterprise was allowed to show what it could do, and a room was let for the nominal rent of £1 per year. Less urgent were the demands of people using the station at Fintown; there one S. offered in May 1899 to run a refreshment room. The Board must have had a pretty clear idea of his intentions, and reading between the lines of the Minutes it is clear that S. was really after free premises to run as a public house. Not unaware of potential trouble at their station if they permitted this, the Board recorded their prohibition of licensed premises at Fintown, though permitting 'a coffee and tea room'. Thwarted in his alcoholic proposals, S. lost interest and Fintown never got its refreshment room.

ON TO DERRY AND TO BALLYSHANNON

In the middle 90s two further extensions to the system were planned, independently of Government help. These were from Strabane to Derry city, and from Donegal to Ballyshannon. Though the first of these duplicated the Great Northern's line, it was felt to be justified since a large part of the Donegal's traffic emanated from Derry. Imported coal was an important part of this. It will be recalled that even when the Finn Valley line was standard gauge, it had been treated as an appendage to the main line. The Donegal Company felt that it was imperative to commence through running. Their only competitor was the Great Northern. The Strabane Canal, opened in 1796, had been allowed to deteriorate and had virtually ceased to carry any traffic, while river-borne shipping on the Foyle had fallen away. For many years, sandbanks had made it impossible

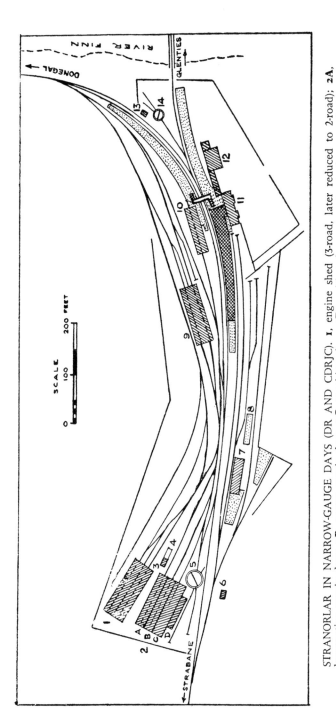

STRANORLAR IN NARROW-GAUGE DAYS (DR AND CDRJC). **1**, engine shed (3-road, later reduced to 2-road); **2A**, locomotive repair shop; **2B**, motor repair shop; **2C**, machine shop; **2D**, smiths' shop; **3**, water tank; **4**, coal store; **5**, turntable (36'); **6**, East signal cabin; **7**, goods store and loading bank; **8**, cattle dock; **9**, carriage and wagon repair shop; **10**, general stores; **11**, station and stationmaster's house; **12**, administrative offices; **13**, West signal cabin; **14**, turntable (20') for railcars to bring coasting craft up-river to the canal mouth, a difficulty emphasised since the 1860s by the limited headroom below the Carlisle Bridge at Derry.

The Donegal-Ballyshannon project was a straightforward tapping of the agricultural lowland country of south-west Donegal. The River Erne formed its natural southern boundary, beyond it to the south the Great Northern ran their long Bundoran branch, and though Ballyshannon was to have two railway stations for its two thousand inhabitants, there was not likely to be direct conflict between the two owning companies.

When application was made in the 1896 Session to build these two lines, the Great Northern Railway, as successor to the L & E and the INW, naturally offered strong opposition to the Strabane— Derry project. However, the 'Donegal Railway Act 1896' received the Royal Assent on 7 August. The Company were empowered to create and issue £100,000 of ordinary share capital, £40,000 of 4 per cent preference shares, and to borrow up to £70,000 as 4 per cent debentures.

Although the management and the operation of the Derry and Ballyshannon branches stemmed from Stranorlar, separate accounts were to be kept of the receipts, as from the Government branches. They were then, as a result of the 1896 Act, treated as nominally a 'Separate Undertaking' for accounting purposes.

The financial arrangements took all of 1897 to complete. It was decided in view of the slow intake of capital, to build the Derry extension first, but it was not until late in 1897 that the Board authorised James Barton to proceed with working plans and drawings. The contract was advertised and in the spring of 1898 was awarded to the London firm of Messrs Topham, Jones & Railton, who started work in the summer, and promised to finish by the end of December 1899.

The course of the Derry extension was necessarily on the east bank of the River Foyle, since the Great Northern's line ran close to the west bank. From Strabane the line was laid as a northerly projection of the existing line, between the river and the GNR metals. After half a mile, it curved towards the latter and passed above them on an embankment. It then bridged in turn a secondary road and the Strabane Canal, and regained a northerly course a short way from the main Strabane—Derry road. It passed through several villages and ended close to the Carlisle Bridge in Derry.

By the end of 1898, Barton's report stated that the contractors had 'brought an excellent supply of plant upon the ground, including two steam navvies'. They were then employing 400 men, and had done work worth £13,000, including 120,000 cubic yards of earthwork and a third of the fencing.

During 1899 work was retarded by a shortage of labour and it became evident that the completion date would have to be put back some months. By the end of December, 17 bridges out of the total of 24 were built and a third of the permanent way was laid. The long embankment across the valley at Strabane had given some trouble due to the soft nature of the subsoil, but this had been overcome. It was expected that the line would be ready by April.

Meanwhile, Messrs Campbell & Son of Belfast were erecting the station buildings. The intermediate stations were simple, one-platform affairs, but the Derry terminus was commodious, a well-designed building, with a broad island platform roofed for most of its length. The city's Port & Harbour Commissioners built a mixed-gauge extension to link the station with their own cross-river line on the Carlisle Bridge and their quayside line to the broad-gauge Waterside Station of the Belfast & Northern Counties Railway, where transhipment facilities were provided.

The Derry extension was opened for goods traffic on 1 August 1900 and for passenger traffic five days later. The line was single throughout, with a passing loop at the intermediate station of Donemana, 6¼ miles from Strabane.

Money for the Ballyshannon extension came in slowly, and after five years the necessary powers had lapsed. The Donegal Railway Act of 23 June 1902 again empowered the Company to make their branch to Ballyshannon. The Act also repealed the requirements of the 1896 Act as to 'Separate Undertakings', and gave the Company powers (none actually used) to work their line by electricity, to build an electrical generating station near Barnesmore station, to subscribe to hotel companies and to the formation of a golf links and Spa Well development near Donegal, and to buy out the Donegal Railway Station Company.

On 14 January 1903, the contract for the construction of the Ballyshannon extension was signed with the firm of Thomas I. Dixon Ltd and shortly afterwards work was begun. It was planned to carry the expanding system towards another part of the Great Northern's territory. The only considerable place on the route was the village of Ballintra, though the magnificent strand at Rossnowlagh offered attractions to holidaymakers provided that the local accommodation could be bettered. The terminus at Ballyshannon was to be on the north side of the town, 'at a point upon the centre line of the wall between Bishop Street in the town of Ballyshannon and a field lying to the north of it now in the occupation of Mrs. Stephens'.

At the end of 1903 the shareholders were told at the half-yearly meeting that more than half of the earthworks and two-thirds of the fencing was done. Dixon was getting a steam digger to work in a large cutting 'at Peg 480' and was using two engines on the line, an old Hunslet 0—4—0 ST named *Isabella* and a new 0—4—0 ST named *Coolmore* which had been bought from Hunslet (No. 1832) and which was delivered at Derry in December 1903. Dixon's work was almost complete by the summer of 1905, and goods traffic began in early September. On 18 September, Major Pringle inspected the line on behalf of the Board of Trade, and two days later formally reported it fit for passenger traffic. The following day, 21 September, the line was opened for passengers.

Since 1893 the Company had possessed nine engines and 28 carriages but with the extension of the track mileage these were not enough. In 1901, the arrival of six new third-class carriages augmented the passenger accommodation by 352 seats. In 1902, Neilson, Reid & Co. supplied two 4—4—4T engines, and two years later Nasmyth, Wilson sent across four 4—6—4T engines, the only examples of the Baltic type on the Irish narrow gauge. The addition of nine more carriages in 1905 brought the coaching stock to a total of 51 vehicles: 13 tricompos, 18 thirds, 12 brake-thirds, five carriage trucks, and three horse boxes.

	Created	Issued	Received
3 per cent Guaranteed stock ...	£201,000	£120,700	£120,700
3 per cent Preference stock ...	£93,644	£93,644	£86,751
Ordinary stock	£127,035	£127,035	£93,957
	£421,679	£341,379	£301,408
Baronial guaranteed shares:			
West Donegal Light Railway (Killybegs) Order 1890	£1,000	£1,000	£1,000
Finn Valley Railway (Stranorlar—Glenties) Order 1891	£1,000	£1,000	£1,000
Total	£423,679	£343,379	£303,408

Page 53: LOCOMOTIVES—1

*(above) No. 2 'Blanche' (Class 1); (centre) No. 4 'Meenglas' (Class 2);
(below) No. 10 'Sir James' (Class 3)*

Page 54: LOCOMOTIVES—2

(above) No. 10 'Owenea' (Class 4) at Strabane, 14 May 1937; (centre) No. 17 'Glenties' (Class 5) at Strabane, 14 May 1937; (below) No. 3 'Lydia' (Class 5a) at Stranorlar, 14 May 1937

Merchandise stock comprised 135 covered wagons, 76 open wagons, 23 ballast wagons, and two brake vans, a total of 236 vehicles.

As seen, the 1902 Act increased the Company's capital, but to meet the growing commitments, Parliamentary sanction was given to further capital expansion. By the end of 1905, the authorised capital of the Company amounted to £640,695, made up of £423,679 of stock and £217,016 of loans and debenture stock. The stock was made up as shown in the table on page 52.

The opening of the Ballyshannon branch lengthened the system to 105½ miles, but it came at a time when the Company's finances had lapsed into their former weakness.

CHAPTER IV

The C.D.R.J.C. 1906-1921

THE MIDLAND AND THE GREAT NORTHERN TAKE-OVER

Since 1903, the Donegal's neighbours at Waterside station in Londonderry had been the Midland Railway of England, who had acquired the old Belfast & Northern Counties Railway, and were administering it through their Northern Counties Committee. The Midland were actively interested in widening their Irish interests, and they offered to purchase the Donegal Railway Company, thereby extending their territory from Belfast, through the Derry stations, into the extreme north-west of Ireland. Their immediate Irish neighbours, the Great Northern, became alarmed at such a prospect, which might have unfavourable long-term consequences. An agreement was reached whereby they and the Midland jointly acquired the Donegal Railway Company. Parliamentary legislation for the purchase was given on 1 May 1906, whereupon the Donegal Railway lost its identity. Administration came under a Board of six members, three from each of the owning companies, and the concern was styled The County Donegal Railways Joint Committee. The administrative offices of the CDRJC continued to be at Stranorlar. The Act of Amalgamation extinguished the Treasury and Baronial guarantees. Ownership of the Strabane—Derry section went wholly to the Midland, but the branch was still worked by the Joint Committee's engines, and their stock was considered to be 'at home' on it.

AN ARDARA SCHEME FAILS

Six miles west of Glenties is Ardara, a small town with a population of around 500. Its size has scarcely altered during the present century. Though close to the coast it has not got the excellent harbour facilities of the port of Killybegs. Lace, embroidery and homespun manufactures provide local employment.

The significance of the opening of the railway to Glenties in 1895 had not been lost on the Ardara people. As an urban community they were comparable in size to Glenties, and the view was held that the sooner the railway was extended beyond Glenties and into Ardara the better. Three years before the Joint Committee was formed, the Government had financed the Burtonport and Carndonagh extensions in north Donegal, and the more hopeful among the Ardara folk were sure that they had only to ask to secure treatment as generous as their northern cousins. It took twenty years to disillusion them.

On 27 February 1903 a petition or 'memorial' was addressed to the Donegal directors, the 29 signatories being headed by the local clergy. Prominent among the supporters were two local businessmen, Michael McNelis and Hugh O'Dwyer. The document claimed that the capital cost would be comparatively small and that a fair return would be certain, though no specific figures were mentioned. The directors were sanguine, they acknowledged the petition and took no further action.

Three years passed and from the 1906 take-over the Ardara people gained fresh hope. An Improvements Committee was formed and a fresh petition was mounted, going this time to the Chief Secretary of the Lord Lieutenant of Ireland. By now, railway management had taken time to ponder the viability of the scheme, and they were not enamoured with it. Unlike the Ardara amateurs, they were in a position to form a shrewd estimate of what the line would earn. In October 1906 Livesey wrote to Plews of the Great Northern : 'If Parliament find the money to make the extension, the Joint Committee would not object to work it.' Neither owning company felt inclined to meet any part of the capital cost, for they had the example of the Burtonport line to guide them.

It was clear that no Government liberality was likely to be offered unless, as a Dublin Castle spokesman put it, 'the County Council and the railway themselves were prepared to make definite and substantial offers'. The honeymoon of full grants was over. In their turn the County Council were not prepared to make the first move, and the Joint Committee reiterated their policy of being prepared to work the line 'if handed over ... fully equipped'. The matter rested there for five years more.

In the summer of 1912, Michael McNelis, by then Clerk to the Rural District Council, rejuvenated the project. Approaches were made for financial help to the Development Commission and to the Congested Districts Board. Under Henry Forbes, a lenient railway attitude was becoming evident, and he and young Livesey even cast a professional eye over the course of the line and reckoned that it could be made for £5,000 a mile at the most, and no additional rolling stock would be needed to work it. For the benefit of the members of the Joint Committee potential traffic was analysed, and shown to be comparatively light. A subscription of £2,000, shared between the Midland and the Great Northern was offered, leaving the promoters to raise the balance of around twelve times that amount. Earnings for the railway would have been around 8 per cent on their small investment, and it was abundantly clear that no adequate return would come from the total sum needed to construct the extension, even though the Congested Districts Board would have given the land free of cost.

Oblivious to the economic hopelessness of the scheme the Ardara promoters persisted. Negotiations were reopened in 1919 and again in 1922. By then the Irish Railways Commission was deliberating in Dublin. On 25 May 1922 Henry Hunt, manager of the Lough Swilly company, was giving evidence. Brimfull of confidence, he suggested that 'the making of a line from Dungloe to Fintown or thereabouts, and from Glenties to Killybegs, if not too costly, would complete the railway facilities of Donegal'. Opening the paper the following morning, Henry Forbes was incensed by what Hunt had said and promptly penned a letter to one of the Ardara supporters:

> You will be aware there is a Commission at present sitting in Dublin, going into the question of the Irish Railways.
>
> From to-day's paper you will see that Mr Henry Hunt, the English Manager of the Londonderry & Lough Swilly Railway, and who I do not suppose ever spent a day in the district, proposed that the Donegal Railway should be extended from Glenties to Killybegs and from Fintown to Dungloe. I need not expound on the folly of such a scheme.
>
> Would it not be well for you to get your local committee together again and present your case to the Commission setting out what you are prepared to do and reviving again the proposed extension from Glenties to Ardara.
>
> If I can assist you in any way I am at your disposal.

A year before, Forbes had closed the Glenties line because of civil disturbances. In his enthusiasm, he was now doing what he could to revitalise the Ardara proposals, and with them the Glenties traffic. But post-war inflation had come, no British assistance was to be expected, and the prospect of having to find over 90 per cent of the capital still confronted the Ardara committee. The problem was even more acute than it had been twenty years before and the

Ardara plans were gently allowed to die, even before competition from road traffic could have crippled them.

THE LINE TO LETTERKENNY

By the beginning of the 20th century 99 miles of 3-ft-gauge railway were being operated by the Londonderry & Lough Swilly Railway, linking Burtonport and Letterkenny with Derry city. Though the administrative headquarters of the L & LS were in Derry, the only physical connection between that system and the Donegal's lines was over the quayside lines of the Harbour Commissioners and across the river by the Carlisle Bridge. On the bridge, a deck below the roadway was laid in mixed gauge rails, with turntables at each end of the bridge. Wagon exchange was possible, but not through running of trains or transfer of coaching stock. The mixed gauge was necessary since the lines on the bridge also connected the broad-gauge systems of the Great Northern and the Belfast & Northern Counties Railways. These companies had termini at Foyle Road and at Waterside, on the west and east banks of the river.

In that part of south-east Donegal that lay between the hinterlands of the two narrow-gauge railways were the small towns of Raphoe and Convoy. At the end of the 19th century Raphoe had a population of around 700, and although little more than a village by cross-channel standards, it was centred around a cathedral, a ruined bishop's palace and a Royal School. Convoy, only about a third the size of Raphoe, was a manufacturing village with a reputation for woollen textile manufacture. By Donegal standards, the people living there felt they ought to have a railway.

Efforts to drive a railway between the River Foyle and Lough Swilly had in fact begun as early as 1860, for had the initial scheme of the Letterkenny Railway not been still-born, it would have formed a link between Cuttymanhill and Pluck. But powerful Derry city interests saw in such a line, the diversion of the traffic from central Donegal that they had enjoyed, and the Letterkenny Railway eventually was persuaded to run from the town of that name to a junction with the L & LSR near Farland Point.* Twenty-five years later came a proposal for either a light railway or a roadside tramway between Strabane and Drumcairn, near Manorcunningham. The idea had the backing of the Marquis of Hamilton and of E. T. Herdman of Sion Mills, and came two years after the completion of

* See Chapter III of THE LOUGH SWILLY RAILWAY

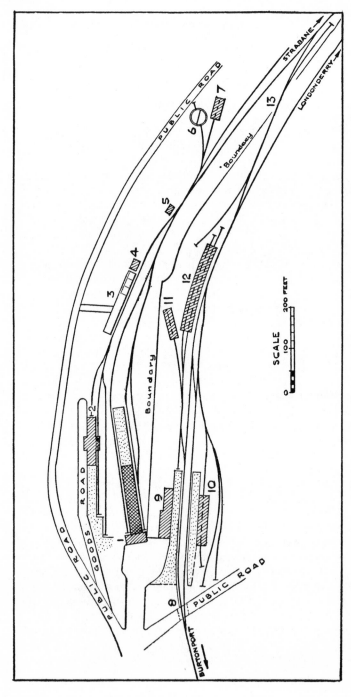

LETTERKENNY. **1**, S & LR passenger station; **2**, goods store; **3**, cattle pens; **4**, signal cabin; **5**, water tank; **6**, turntable (42'); **7**, engine shed; **8**, road level crossing (L & LSR); **9**, L & LSR passenger station (originally Letterkenny Rly.); **10**, L & LSR goods store; **11**, L & LSR engine shed (turntable later sited in front); **12**, L & LSR carriage shed; **13**, connecting spur between S & LR and L & LSR

the Letterkenny Railway. The new scheme had been examined by John Barton as consultant, and he estimated that a tramway via Raphoe would cost £44,000, while a light railway via Ballindrait would require £60,000 of capital. There was enthusiasm for a time, and then the idea lapsed for lack of money.

The next revival of interest took the form of a railway from Strabane to Letterkenny. In September 1902, a meeting of the promoters and the public took place in Lifford Court House. For the 14 miles of line, routed by Lifford, Ballindrait, Convoy and Raphoe, James Barton gave the cost as £100,000. With the Boer War in mind, James Donnell of Strabane rose to support the motion and said that when Lord Kitchener, after his experiences in South Africa, had wished to reach Letterkenny, he soon found that the best way to do so was by motor car. The speaker looked on that as a good argument for the necessity for the proposed railway.

During the winter of 1902-3 the scheme got off the ground, and preparations were made to submit a Bill to Parliament. Rather surprisingly, Derry Corporation resolved not to oppose the Bill in Parliament, and it was duly deposited. Once there however, strenuous opposition was offered to it by John McFarland of the firm of McCrea & McFarland of Derry, who handled much of the cartage between the railway stations and the docks. His objections were reinforced by those of the Lough Swilly Railway, and as a result the scheme was restricted during its passage through parliament, and emerged as the Strabane, Raphoe and Convoy Railway Act, with powers to build a railway link between these places alone, and not to Letterkenny. The Derry objectors had been appeased.

In spite of this setback, proponents of the Strabane-Letterkenny line did not relax their efforts. In November 1903, the Great Northern Railway promised to advance £72,000 to construct and equip the complete line, and support came from resolutions passed at public meetings in Burtonport and Dungloe in the west of the county. A further application was made to Parliament, and in July 1904 permission was given to extend the line beyond Convoy to Letterkenny, and to change the name of the company to the Strabane & Letterkenny Railway.

In advance of their take-over of the Donegal Railway, the GNR(I) and the Midland in February 1905 promoted a Bill which would have permitted them to assume virtual ownership of the S & LR. That company were to make an agreement with the Great Northern to work and maintain their line, receiving £3 10s per mile per week, while the Great Northern retained between 50 per cent and 60 per cent of the receipts. The Great Northern were to put up £60,000 of the capital, leaving only £28,000 to be raised by the nominal owners. The Bill went forward in June 1905 only to have the Commons Committee insert a clause protecting the Port of Derry, and as a result the promoters withdrew their Bill.

There was still no progress with construction, and during the summer of 1905, rumours circulated that the entire project had been abandoned. These proved to be false, however, and at last in March 1906, work started on making the railway. The main contractors were Robert McAlpine & Sons, with Courtney & Co. making the stations. At the Letterkenny end, the line passed over that of the Letterkenny Railway and, turning towards the west, ran in alongside it to a terminus that was beside that of the older line. The making of the s & L station necessitated the diversion of the county road for some distance.

Shortly after work had begun, there was a strike on the Ballindrait section, where the workmen were being paid half a crown for a day of ten hours. In April, it was reported in the local press that a small locomotive had arrived at Letterkenny for the contractors, indicating that construction was being progressed from both ends of the line and that the ballast engine had been brought over the Swilly's Letterkenny line. McAlpine used four engines during the construction: two came as new engines from Hudswell, Clarke (*Strabane* in 1907 and *Donegal* in 1908, an 0—6—0T and an 0—4—2ST) and they bought two engines from Dixon's Ballyshannon contract (*Coolmore* and *Isabella*).

At the 7th half-yearly meeting of the s & LR, in August 1907, good progress was reported and half of the permanent way was stated to have been laid. By the following spring, the track was complete enough to allow the running of a special train for the directors and officials on 17 April 1908. But enough had still to be done to delay the opening for the rest of that year. Meanwhile, the Lough Swilly company held their half-yearly meeting on 24 August, and the chairman, John McFarland, continued his criticism of the scheme, calling it

> a wild-cat speculative scheme promoted by local men to the disadvantage of local industries which were at a low enough ebb. ...The capital expenditure he took roughly at £150,000 for construction and equipment. The entire traffic of the existing railway, Londonderry to Letterkenny, for the past year was £8,433. Assuming that half of that traffic was lost to that company by competition with their powerful neighbours—the Midland and Great Northern—who were joint owners of the new line, and that was assuming a great deal,

the remaining half, say £4,200 a year, would not pay the wages of the staff and maintenance of the new line. Consequently, those who supplied the capital of £150,000 would never get one penny of interest on their money. . . .

Final completion of the line was delayed some months due to difficulties over the entry of the line to Strabane and after the Board of Trade inspection had been completed, the line was opened for traffic on New Year's Day 1909. The *Londonderry Sentinel* devoted two columns to a description of the scene. The first train left Strabane at 10.10 a.m., ten minutes late, and was headed by No. 20 *Raphoe*.

Since much of the share capital of the s & l had been provided by the Midland and the Great Northern, owners of the CDRJC since 1906, it was natural that the Joint Committee should take over the operation of the line, and work it as a branch. Nominally the s & l possessed three locomotives, 18 coaches and 50 wagons, but their acquisition was merely a paper transaction, as they were transferred from the CDRJC's book stock and continued to bear that company's livery. The s & l issued separate reports and issued tickets headed 's & LR'. With the opening of the Letterkenny branch, the total mileage of the narrow-gauge system worked by the Joint Committee rose to its maximum of $124\frac{1}{2}$; of this 91 miles were directly owned by the Joint Committee, the Strabane & Letterkenny accounted for $19\frac{1}{4}$ miles, and $14\frac{1}{2}$ miles were the property of the Midland Railway.

THE LIVESEYS AND LAWSON

From 1890 until 1897, R. H. Livesey had been secretary, accountant and locomotive superintendent, at first of the Finn Valley and West Donegal companies, and then of the Donegal Railway Co. In May 1897, Edward Radcliff ended his engagement as resident engineer and was not replaced; his duties were, however, taken over by Livesey, though the Certificates in the half-yearly reports were signed by Abraham Stewart. At the same time, Livesey relinquished a part of his varied responsibilities on the appointment of W. R. Lawson, who came from the City of Glasgow Union Railway to be the Donegal's secretary and accountant. Simultaneously, Livesey was elevated to the status of general manager, though retaining as we have seen his direct interest in both civil and mechanical engineering matters.

By 1906 Livesey's retirement was imminent, and at the October meeting of the Committee the whole staff position was reviewed.

The family name of Livesey was to continue in association with the line for another 16 years, for R. M. Livesey was ready to take over where his father had left off. From 1 November 1906 'young Livesey', as he is still spoken of at Stranorlar, was made superintendent of permanent way and chief of the locomotive department, and from 1 January 1907 (the date on which his father finally severed his ties with the railway) traffic superintendent as well.

The staff of the CDRJC at the end of 1906 was listed as follows:

	Salary
W. R. Lawson, secretary and accountant	£350
R. M. Livesey, supt. of p. way and chief of loco. dept. ...	£300
D. Bogle, chief clerk	£150
C. W. Wheatley, rates clerk	£130
J. Shields, chief audit clerk	£150
P. Whitelaw, audit clerk	£110
5 clerks ... ... totalling	£286
46 stationmasters and station clerks ... totalling	£2,674

The stationmasters were paid salaries of between £75 and £110; it was remarked in 1909 that the Ballyshannon stationmaster was receiving £110 and was 'grossly overpaid'.

Under the new management, and guided and backed by the owning companies, certain changes ensued. A concession whereby county councillors attending County Council meetings were provided with return tickets at single fare was stopped, but it was decided not to discontinue a like concession to the Sisters of Charity. In November 1906 it was decided to spend £16 on the purchase of a quadricycle for the use of the Stranorlar permanent-way inspector, and to purchase for the secretary a 'typewriting machine'. The latter item must have speedily justified itself for a second one was ordered for Livesey's department in January 1907. The workshops at Stranorlar were then attended to: while they had been sufficient to deal with light locomotive repairs, it had been the practice to send very heavy repairs to the makers. Henceforward they were to be done at the shops of the owning companies. It appears indeed that the facilities until then had been of the simplest, for in February 1907 tenders were accepted for a radial drilling machine, screwing machine, emery grinder, planing machine, hack saw, 7 in. and 12 in. lathes, and an 8½ in. slotting machine. The total cost was £557.

The permanent way also received attention, in particular the original West Donegal section through the Gap, which was urgently in need of relaying. Heavier rails were put in, and by August 1908 it was declared to be fit to accept the two 4—4—4 T engines. These had been bought in 1902, but had been prohibited west of Stranorlar by reason of their high axle loading of nearly 11 tons.

The rolling stock was increased. Five engines, all 2—6—4 T type, came from Nasmyth Wilson in 1907-08, bringing the stock of engines from the Patricroft works to nine. Although Charles Clifford, as the GNR locomotive superintendent, had surveillance over the CDRJC engines, it is interesting to note that the first Nasmyth Wilson engines to be added to the 5-ft 3-in.-gauge GNR stock did not come until 1911, by which time they would have proved themselves on the narrow gauge. New carriages and wagons were also added to the stock in 1907.

The Committee's coal supplies were next to come under notice. At the end of 1906, an order had been placed for the supply of 6,000 tons of coal at 18s 6d per ton, with delivery over the next 12 months. By September 1908, a mysterious stock shortage of 537 tons was discovered. The loss represented nearly a month's supply of fuel and immediate measures were taken to regularise and improve weighing and stocktaking methods.

DONEGAL FOR TOURISTS

The potential attractions of Donegal to tourists had been realised for some years but its expansion had been slowed by the lack of good hotel accommodation. In the earliest days of the Finn Valley, accommodation for visitors was comparatively primitive. An 1875 tourist guide book* to the North of Ireland commented in the chapter headed 'The Donegal Highlands': 'The traveller will not expect, of course, to find the same accommodation in the way of hotels and coaches here as in the more populous parts of the island. . . .'

Though the 1902 Act of Parliament gave them the necessary powers, unlike the other railways in the north of Ireland, the Donegal Railway Company had no spare capital or profits to divert to the building or supporting of hotels, much though they might be needed to augment traffic. A similar policy seems to have continued under the Joint Committee, though with two hotel-owning companies behind the Donegal line one can detect a certain leaning towards the innkeeping business. Thus in April 1907, the Minutes

* *Guide to Belfast, The Giant's Causeway and the North of Ireland*, pub. A. & C. Black, Edinburgh.

mention briefly a report that Fintra House was 'quite unsuitable for a hotel'.

In November 1911 it was decided to contribute £10 towards the estimated expenditure of £35 on the new golf links at Rossnowlagh.

Expansion was left to private enterprise until June 1913, when there is reference to consideration of making an hotel in 'the Donegal Highlands between Gweedore and Bundoran'. At the same meeting at which this was minuted, the Committee declined to buy the Lough Veagh Hotel, near Church Hill, doubtless since it was well within L & LS territory. A year later the country was on the brink of war and hotel-keeping was put aside for more serious matters.

Around 1900, tourism was stimulated by the issue of a *Tourist Programme* by the Committee. This was similarly sized to their public timetables and was a well-written and plentifully-illustrated booklet containing around 20 pages of text, backed by twice that amount of advertising matter. The *Tourist Programme*, revised each year, was issued as a free supplement to the timetables, and after about 1910 both showed on their covers attractive, composite, half-tone illustrations of local scenery, a maker's photograph of one of their Baltic locomotives, and the Joint Committee's coat-of-arms. About 1914 the illustrated covers were replaced by more sober ones, but the contents were clearly and carefully written to encourage tourists and especially those from 'across the water'. The phrase 'The Donegal Highlands' was successfully coined and was reiterated to drive home the genuine similarity of the scenery and sporting facilities to those offered in the Scottish Highlands.

REORGANIZATION UNDER FORBES

In 1909, when the system operated by the CDRJC attained its full size, the spacing of the stations and halts reflected to some extent the variations in the density of population. An average distance of almost exactly two miles separated stopping places on the Finn Valley, Killybegs, Ballyshannon and Derry sections; on the Strabane and Letterkenny section the distance was 2½ miles and on the West Donegal section 3½ miles. Apart from the five termini and the three junction stations, none of the places served was of any great size, and it says much for the efficiency of operation under Henry Forbes, who had come from the GNR to succeed W. R. Lawson in 1910, that not only were the original stations and halts practically all in existence up to the closure of their respective lines but quite a few halts were opened subsequently. Furthermore, a large number of supplementary request stops were introduced, principally at the numerous level crossings with roads and lanes.

There was, however, one contrary move, when in 1907 it was proposed to close Ballybofey station. This was the first station out on the Glenties line, but was only half a mile from Stranorlar. Of the twin towns that faced the Finn, Ballybofey contained the majority of the shops and, as might have been anticipated, the local merchants raised their voices in vigorous protest. At the Committee meeting on 21 March it was decided to leave Ballybofey open 'meantime', and probably because the ensuing uncertainty drew further protests it was resolved on 5 September 1907 'that Ballybofey be not closed'.

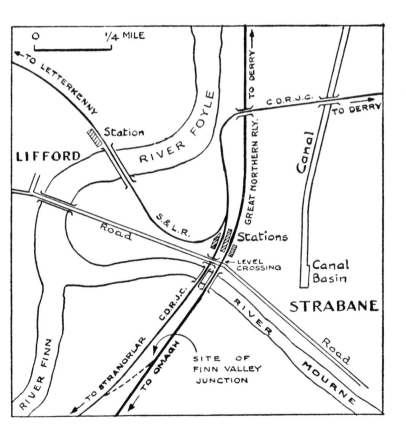

Under Forbes's superintendence there was a prompt realization of the benefits to traffic that would result by an increase in the number of stopping places. On 24 August 1910, the Committee resolved to inspect a possible site for a halt at Cornagillagh, between Convoy and Letterkenny, and a platform, three carriages in length, was opened there on 1 August 1911. In June 1914 it was extended to twice its original length.

On 1 August 1911, Creevy Halt was opened, 2¾ miles from Ballyshannon. Earlier in the year, the Glenties branch received a halt at Shallogans, nearly midway in the long section between Fintown and Glenties. Then in June 1912 a petition was read from residents near the head of the Barnesmore Gap, for a halt to be made for accommodation when markets were being held at Donegal and Ballybofey. Their prayers did not go unheard and Derg Bridge Halt was opened on 2 December 1912.

To come into line with the parent companies, in 1908 the stations were graded from first to fourth class, with responsibilities, work and wages fixed accordingly. Only Letterkenny, Stranorlar and Donegal qualified for the élite first class. The 'Agents'' uniforms were graded, first and second class being provided with jacket suits, third class with the same outfit but with less trimming, and fourth class agents with a blue cloth jacket and vest and corduroy trousers. All wore caps. The estimated cost of providing uniforms was £60 a year.

Evidence of the growth in freight traffic was to be seen by the building of new goods offices at Donegal at a cost of £65 in 1913, and at Glenties at a cost of £70 in 1915, while a store costing £16 was erected at Clady in 1916.

Strabane shed was originally wooden. A severe storm in November 1911 damaged it severely, and as repairs would have cost around £120, it was decided to replace it. Drawings were prepared in January 1912 for a two-road shed, also of wood, 83 ft 3 in. in length and 29 ft in width, and it was completed and brought into use in the following July.

Modernisation was seen at Stranorlar station when acetylene lighting was provided in 1912 at a cost of £547. About the same time carriage lighting by acetylene gas began to be introduced.

What were to be the final additions to the locomotive stock came in 1912. Livesey was well satisfied with the nine Nasmyth, Wilson engines already on the books and he decided to go again to them for three more 2—6—4 tanks, differing only in detail from the five that had come in 1907-08. In the same year two of the

three original West Donegal engines were scrapped, after having
been withdrawn for some time. With the arrival of the new engines
the locomotive stock rose to its maximum of 21, and it remained
thus for a period of 14 years.

THE FIRST WORLD WAR

The outbreak of World War I in August 1914 found the CDRJC
in excellent fettle and well prepared to carry on business in spite
of depletion of staff, decreasing tourist traffic and rising costs of
working. Wages and fuel bills accounted for much of the increased
operating costs. Coal cost 20s 3d per ton in 1913, by 1916 it was
33s 6d and by 1918 42s. It rose to 74s 2d in 1921, but then fell
back to around half of that peak figure.

Wages remained fairly steady until 1917, but rose rapidly thereafter to between three and four times their pre-war totals. Then
from 1 January 1917 until 17 August 1921, Government control
was imposed on all the Irish railways, through the medium of the
Irish Railways Executive Committee.

On a railway such as the Donegal, an engineer with a gift for
improvisation and an inventive turn of mind was doubly useful in
wartime, and R. M. Livesey was one such. In July 1915 he reported
to the Committee that he had devised a reinforced, longitudinal
concrete sleeper which he claimed would satisfactorily replace the
imported pine variety. The Committee referred the invention to
Bowman Malcolm, who as the Northern Counties Committee
engineer was the senior official responsible for permanent-way
upkeep, but he did not feel inclined to adopt them and the proposal
was shelved.

What might have been an interesting sideline at the Stranorlar
workshops was brought up at the meeting of the Committee on
22 September 1915. The war was well into its stride and military
requirements were outpacing production in some directions. The
Joint Committee authorised Livesey to make a sample supply of
cases for Mills Hand Grenades for the Belfast Employers' Munitions
Committee. Search of the Minutes does not reveal any further
mention of the manufacture of grenades and it seems likely that
production could not be undertaken because of the lack of facilities
for ferrous casting.

At the instigation of the Irish Railways Executive Committee
the Stranorlar workshops opened their doors in April 1917 to one
of the engines which the L & LS were using to work their Burtonport

line. This was No. 6, one of the two heavy Hudswell, Clarke 4—8—4 tanks that had been bought in 1912. The engine, which was badly needed to maintain services, was brought across to Stranorlar for general heavy repairs and boiler work. The inadequacy of the L & LS rolling stock was seen again in 1921 when by order of the IREC it was augmented by the loan of five of the Joint Committee's carriages. The Joint Committee learnt on 21 September 1921 that two of them had been returned and instructed Forbes to press for the return of the others. These came back during the following month, and the Clearing House was told to credit the Joint Committee with the sum of 6s per day for the period of loan.

The Irish Railways Executive Committee also negotiated the loan of the remaining one of the West Donegal engines, *Alice*, to the Cork, Blackrock & Passage Railway from 1918 until 1921.

The main feature of Government control was that the CDRJC, in common with the other companies, received no direct payment for services to the Government such as the transport of military personnel and stores, but the Government guaranteed them the same net earnings as those of 1913. Inflated costs complicated the picture. Not until the railways emerged from their period of control, almost three years after the end of the war, did the Government pay a cash sum as compensation for services rendered and towards arrears of maintenance. The Irish Railways received a block grant of £3m, and of this the share given to the CDRJC was £60,613, paid in equal instalments in 1922-3-4.

Page 71: RAILCARS—1

(above) Railcar No. 1, in 1926. Mr Parks, locomotive foreman at Stranorlar, on left; Mr Glover, locomotive engineer of Great Northern Railway (Ireland) on right; (below) Railcar No. 2, in 1926. Mr Forbes on left, Mr Ross Parks on right

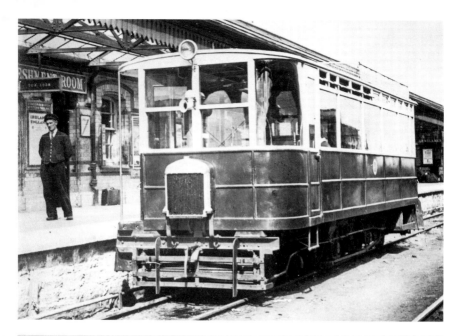

Page 72: RAILCARS—2

Drewry petrol railcar No. 3 ex-D & BST at Strabane, 1935; (below)
Double-headed mixed train at Ballintra. Railcar No. 6 piloting No. 7,
with three vans in rear

CHAPTER V

The C.D.R.J.C. 1921-1960

THE UNEASY PEACE

Before Government control had released its hold on the system, the Committee were faced with the overdue task of bringing their rolling stock and permanent way up to the high standards that had existed before 1914. The task was complicated and frustrated by the changing political scene in Ireland. British rule was coming to an end, and the country was divided into two separate self-governing parts in 1921. Twenty-six counties formed the Irish Free State, the remaining six Northern Ireland. So far as this division affected the CDRJC, County Donegal joined the Free State, while Counties Tyrone and Derry went to form part of Northern Ireland. Much of the system was therefore in the Free State, and only the Derry branch was completely in Northern Ireland. The line crossed the inter-state frontier in two places, on the FVR section at Urney Bridge and on the Strabane & Letterkenny section at the Lifford Bridge.

Internal tensions and civil disorders marked the period before and after the formation of the Free State, and from 1921 until 1923 a state of civil war existed there. Inevitably the railways became a favoured target for acts of sabotage. The first serious incidents which affected the CDRJC took place in the spring of 1920 and they continued intermittently for three years. Many of the minor, if more personal, incidents went unrecorded, either officially in the Minute Books or correspondence, or publicly in the newspapers, but the following extracts from the first two sources illustrate the extremely trying and often dangerous conditions under which the officers and staff worked for almost three years.

> 1920 15 April: Obstructions and delays to trains on the Ballyshannon branch. Overbridge damaged by explosives. Telegraph and block wires cut.
>
> 23 July: Armed raiders searched and held two trains for Post Office mails, the 8.15 a.m. ex Ballyshannon at Bridgetown and the 7.55 a.m. ex Strabane at Ballinamore.

THE COUNTY DONEGAL RAILWAYS
JOINT COMMITTEE.

PUBLIC NOTICE

On the Night of Wednesday, 17th November, 1920,
AT INVER STATION,

a Guard of this Railway was dragged from his Van by cowardly masked and armed ruffians; he was handcuffed, was placed against a wall, revolvers were presented at him, and his life was threatened if he continued to carry on the duties for which he is paid.

In consequence of this outrage on an inoffensive Railwayman, the train service on the Killybegs Line will be restricted at an early date, and if further interference with the Railway Staff takes place—in the absence of Military protection—the line between Donegal and Killybegs will be

CLOSED.

HENRY FORBES, Traffic Manager.

STRANORLAR

No. 2906 22 11 20

Relic of The Troubles. A wall poster, 18″ x 23″, printed in black on white, which was issued shortly after the incident at Inver

1920 *24 August*: Raiders held and searched the 9.0 a.m. train ex
contd.   Stranorlar at Cloghan.
      6 September: Raiders held and searched 10.30 a.m. train ex
              Donegal at Bridgetown.
      8 September: Raiders held and searched 4.5 p.m. train ex
              Ballyshannon at Drumbar.
              (The Committee closed Bridgetown and Drumbar halts
              for some time on 15 September as a result of these two
              raids.)
      11 November: 8.0 a.m. train ex Killybegs detained for three
              hours as the driver refused to work. (The train was to
              carry British military personnel.)
      15 November: S & L section reopened. (It had been closed since
              30 July.) Military protection given to trains.
      16 November: 9.0 a.m. train ex Stranorlar held up by raiders
              at Ballinamore.
      17 November: Train due at Inver at 5.30 p.m. held up. Guard
              threatened with death by armed men.
1921 *20 February*: Train derailed between Fintown and Glenties due
              to malicious damage to track. The train ran down the
              embankment into Lough Finn.
      14 April: Rail removed and telegraph wires cut near 24½ m.p.
              on Glenties branch.
      15 April: Glenties station broken into by armed men. Telegraph
              and block wires cut. The line was immediately closed
              by order of the manager.
      10 May: Track broken and pulled out of place at 33¾ m.p.
              near Shallogans.
      11 May: Water-tank house and cabin at Fintown station
              wrecked and tools stolen. A 27-ft length of rail was
              removed near Cloghan station, carried 200 yd and thrown
              into a river.
      13 May: Explosives used to damage an iron girder bridge over
              Stranabrattoge River near Fintown.
      30 May: Fifty yd of track torn up at 26 m.p. in Glassaghmore
              townland, between Cloghan and Ballinamore, carried
              away and thrown into the bed of a nearby river.
      8 June: Mountcharles, Inver and Dunkineely stations raided by
              masked and armed men. Telegraph and E.T.S. apparatus
              damaged. (As a result, the Killybegs line was closed for
              6 days.)
      20 June: Three hundred yd of track and sleepers torn up near
              24½ m.p., Cronadun townland between Cloghan and
              Ballinamore. Four crossing gates torn from their fasten-
              ings in the same district.
      29 June: About 100 yd of track pulled up in Currynanerriagh
              townland, near Fintown. Length of rail lifted at Meenglas.
      20 July: Four rails pulled out in Meenasrone North townland,
              Glenties branch. Rails pulled out, sleepers, bolts and
              fastenings stolen and gradient posts destroyed, Boughna-
              bradden townland, Glenties branch.
      25 July: Glenties branch reopened.

THE COUNTY DONEGAL RAILWAYS

JOINT COMMITTEE.

PUBLIC NOTICE.

On SATURDAY, 26th FEBRUARY, 1921,

a number of large boulders were placed on the Railway near Ballinamore
Station on the

STRANORLAR & GLENTIES LINE

to obstruct the passage of Trains, and on the same day, and at a point between
Fintown and Glenties, a rail was removed, the track was torn up, and so
diverted as to result in a Train being thrown off the Line and precipitated
down the embankment into the lake alongside. From information received it
is clear this was the work of miscreants living in the immediate vicinity.

The action of the cowardly criminals who perpetrated the above might
have caused a calamitous accident, and involved the death of the Railwaymen
concerned with the working of the Train, as well as the Passengers, and this is
to give Notice that if there is any further interference with the Railway the

STRANORLAR AND GLENTIES LINE

WILL BE

CLOSED

For **ALL TRAFFIC** without further Notice.

Any information that will lead to the identification of the guilty parties will
be thankfully received by the undersigned.

HENRY FORBES, Traffic Manager.

STRANORLAR.

26-2-21.

1922 *18 February*: Stationmaster's office at Ballintra broken into and safe removed. The safe was later found in a field a mile away, undamaged.

28 June: Wagon of locomotive coal for Letterkenny Shed seized by armed men and taken off the 5.35 p.m. train ex Strabane at Raphoe. The contents of the wagon were then taken away.

7 July: E.T.S. and telegraph wires cut at 16½ m.p., Dromore townland near Letterkenny.

24 July: Seven telegraph poles cut down between Convoy and Glenmaquin and about a mile of telegraph wire torn away.

31 July: Porter W. held up by armed men at Mountcharles and robbed of £19 16s 10d, being the amount he had collected from traders for freight.

14 August: E.T.S. and telegraph wires cut at 16¾ m.p., Dromore townland near Letterkenny.

22 August: Castlefinn signal cabin burned maliciously.

6 September: Clady station wrecked by armed men. Goods store set on fire and partly destroyed.

16 October: Booking office at Fintown station broken into and telephone apparatus smashed.

1923 *2 February*: Armed men entered Mountcharles ticket office and compelled the stationmaster to hand over all the cash on hand, amounting to £2 2s 3d.

Through the period of 'The Troubles' Forbes was a tower of strength to his railway. Although his own political views were such as to place his life in danger, he was devoid of personal fear and he vigorously opposed any attempts to intimidate his men or to interfere with railway operating. On the occasion of the armed hold-up at Drumbar on 8 September 1920, Forbes happened to be a passenger and saw the train crew held at gun-point by the raiders. He quietly slipped out of the carriage on to the ballast, and reached the engine unobserved. Swiftly clambering up, he produced a revolver from his pocket and threatened to shoot the raiders if they did not leave his men alone. Shots were exchanged, Forbes chased the raiders across a cornfield, caught one of them who had tripped, and led his captive back to the train. The interrupted journey to Donegal was then resumed, Forbes meanwhile keeping the prisoner covered with his revolver. No police could be found on arrival at Donegal, so Forbes transferred himself and his man to the Londonderry train and had a telephone message sent to Stranorlar to have an escort awaiting the train on its arrival. The prisoner was subsequently brought to trial in Londonderry on 28 September 1920.

As the catalogue of incidents indicates, it was the Glenties branch

The County Donegal Railways.

COMFORTS FOR TRAVELLERS!

NEW TEA ROOM
STRANORLAR STATION.

For the convenience of the Travelling Public, a Tea Room will be opened at Stranorlar Station, on Monday, 16th October, 1922, where:—

TEA,   COCOA,
COFFEE,   BOVRIL,

and Light Refreshments may be had at

MODERATE PRICES.

Nothing will be left undone by the Lady in Charge to make the enterprise a success, and she hopes by promptitude, efficiency and courtesy to all classes to secure and retain the support and patronage of the general public.

☞ **No Strong Drink Stocked or Supplied**

Kee & Sons. Printers, Donegal.

Handbill dated October 1922 advertising the opening of a Tea Room at Stranorlar station. Printed in black on green, size 5½" x 8½"

that was interfered with most often, in spite of the fact that a detachment of military were stationed in the workhouse at Glenties, or more likely because of it. In contrast, neither the Derry nor the s & L roads were cut.

REHABILITATION

Before the civil disturbances had ended, R. M. Livesey resigned, leaving for India in July 1922 after 16 years with the Company. In his place there was appointed on a temporary basis S. F. Jones, who for a time around 1910 had been Livesey's engineering assistant and in the interim had been with the GNR.

Relations between Jones and Forbes were never easy and in under three months Jones left. It was then decided that his post should devolve on the engineers of the two parent companies, W. K. Wallace, engineer and locomotive superintendent of the Northern Counties Committee, and G. T. Glover, locomotive engineer of the GNR. Technical details involving rolling stock and engines were referred to Glover at Dundalk, while matters regarding the permanent way and buildings were dealt with by Wallace at Belfast. At the same time the executive organisation of the CDRJC was altered and Forbes was given intermediary disciplinary control of all departments. At Stranorlar, the responsibilities of chief foreman Parks were widened.

As on every railway, occasional incidents took place which for a time disturbed the even tenor of the quiet countryside. In March 1910 it was reported that G., one of the station clerks, had absconded, taking with him £15 from the till. The police issued a warrant for G.'s arrest but he apparently got away, for nothing further was minuted regarding either him or the £15.

Nine years later, at Donegal station, a drunken man, N.K., made an unprovoked assault on Porter Pat Curran. Curran in defending himself gave K. a push. It must have been well directed for K. fell and sustained injuries from which he subsequently died. Curran was arrested on a charge of murder, but was afterwards admitted to bail. He was committed to trial at the Lifford Assizes in March 1920 but was found not guilty.

Now and then, too, the Minutes recorded sad accidents to trespassers, two of them towards the end of 1913 to old men : one killed by a train near Strabane in November, and another killed a month later at Donegal. In those days of rutted roads, the well-kept ballast of the railway might have been easier walking, but for the old and hard-of-hearing a dangerous route. A similar tragedy occurred on a winter's night alongside Stranorlar platform, when in December 1915 a cattle dealer, McC., was found badly injured after the arrival of the 6.20 p.m. train from Glenties.

NEIGHBOUR RELATIONS

Although the CDRJC and the Londonderry & Lough Swilly Railway were operating narrow-gauge lines in the same county, they appear to have had remarkably few business dealings. Until the S & L section was built this is not surprising, since the only physical contact between the two was over the dockside lines of the Londonderry Harbour Commissioners. In January 1909, however, they found themselves cheek-by-jowl in Letterkenny and thenceforward they could scarcely afford to ignore each other's existence. A letter came to Stranorlar in the following July: it appeared that one of the Lough Swilly trains had killed a cow at a level crossing, an occurrence certainly not peculiar to the Lough Swilly. But it transpired that the owners of the late cow regarded the level crossing as an unusual one, and anxious for full compensation for their loss, held that the crossing was a public right-of-way. This fact the Lough Swilly disputed, and asked the CDRJC to assist in preparing evidence with which to fight a test case in the Court. The Joint Committee, perhaps confident in their superior knowledge of the finer points of level crossings, declined to participate.

The repair of the locomotive and the loan of carriages, made during the exigency of war and at the behest of the IREC, can hardly be interpreted as evidence of any degree of friendliness between the two managements, and perusal of the timetables and the *Tourist Guides* lends support to this, since each company virtually ignored the existence of the other. Through bookings from one line to the other were apparently unknown, though both concerns listed arrangements made with the main-line companies both in Ireland and in England. The L & LS had, in the 14 years prior to 1916, no less than five general managers, eight engineers and nine locomotive superintendents: this history of discontinuity in management probably had much to do with the Donegal's apparent coldness. The contrast between the two concerns was considerable until the arrival in 1916 of Henry Hunt, from the English Great Central, brought stability to the L & LS.

An interesting correspondence was exchanged between the two companies towards the end of 1922. Ten years after their purchase of the two massive 4—8—4 tanks, Henry Hunt of the L & LS was contemplating the addition of 'several new engines' to his stock. The good work of the Nasmyth Wilson 2—6—4 tanks on the Donegal had been noticed, and Hunt and his locomotive superintendent Napier felt that they had much to learn. How much faster could they arrive at a wise decision if they could observe how one of the Donegal's 2—6—4 tanks performed over the Burtonport road? Protocol was observed, and in September Hunt approached G. T. Glover at Dundalk suggesting the experiment. Glover, formally at least, regarded it as 'entirely a matter for arrangement between Messrs. Forbes and Jones of the County Donegal Railway and yourself, as it is purely a question of working, which does not come under my purview'. A fortnight later Hunt wrote to Forbes:

> . . . . it has occurred to me that it would be very desirable, if it is at all possible, that any new engines purchased by us as a three foot gauge line might be standardised with those in use on your Company. . . . I have a section drawing of these engines, but, before moving any further in the matter, I was wondering whether it would be possible for one of these engines to have a trial run over our line, say, from Derry to Burtonport. If this could be done I would be very glad as it would give us a better idea than anything else as to their suitability for our requirements.

Hunt's letter, dated 26 September 1922, shows how the Londonderry & Lough Swilly were regretting their own multiplicity of designs, for at that time they had 19 engines of eight different types.

Forbes's reply on 3 October epitomises delightfully both his own concern with the civil troubles of the period and Stranorlar's traditional lack of confidence in anything pertaining to 'The Swilly'. He wrote:

> I am afraid that I have not sufficient authority to sanction the sending of one of our engines off our own Line, particularly at present. If I were to take this authority on myself, it might happen that we would never get the engine back again, by a combination of circumstances in which the Irregulars of Burtonport and the Bogs of Dungloe would play their respective parts, and as you are gifted with a lively imagination, I leave you to judge the figure I would cut in explaining the circumstances to my Directors. I will, however, place the matter before my Board at their first Meeting, and will acquaint you at once with their decision.

Hunt, no whit abashed, hastened to reassure Forbes and his Board:

> I do not think there is very much danger, if any, in your engine

going to Burtonport. Certainly, we have had nothing happen to our engines for months and months, and, as you know, it is quite an ordinary practice between railway companies for trial runs of this description to take place, and is one which we ourselves would readily agree if asked.

In spite of it all, however, the Joint Committee felt that 'in the present circumstances, it is not considered advisable to comply with your request, but . . . facilities will readily be given to the representatives of your Company to test the engine you are particularly interested in over the Joint Committee's line. . . .'

The history of the Londonderry & Lough Swilly Railway is both colourful and complex for such a comparatively small concern, but this is no place to enlarge upon it, other than to mention contacts with the CDRJC. Suffice to say that the L & LS carried on in a strange blend of dividends and parsimony until rocketing expenditure hit them while they were under Government control. In spite of grants-in-aid from both the Northern and the Free State Governments they made a net loss in 1925, 1926 and 1927. In December 1927 they wrote to the CDRJC requesting that their line be taken over and worked by the Joint Committee. As a result, No. 3 railcar, driven by Ross Parks, was used to convey the Committee on a tour of inspection of the entire L & LS system. Careful consideration was given to the proposal and with central workshop facilities the unified system might well have become a paying concern, at least for a time. But by 1928 the menace of road competition was becoming very real and in the March of that year the Joint Committee formally resolved not to enter into negotiations with the L & LS with a view to working their railway for them. A request from the Northern Government in 1930 that the Committee reconsider their decision was turned down. Thus faded for good the last prospect of a narrow-gauge system of 223½ miles being operated as a unified concern in the north-west of Ireland.

Some years later, when James Whyte had succeeded Hunt as the L & LS general manager, Forbes did actually organise one or two steam-hauled excursions from his line on to Whyte's. These ran through Letterkenny as far as Kilmacrenan, in connection with pilgrimages to Doon Well. The last of these specials was on Sunday, 17 September 1939: it left Killybegs at 7.50 a.m. and arrived in Letterkenny at 11.35 a.m. At 1.15 p.m., still hauled by a Donegal engine, it ran on to Kilmacrenan, 12¼ miles away, returning from there at 4.30 p.m. for Letterkenny.

The Urney Bridge, linking Tyrone and Donegal a short way east of Clady station, has been mentioned already. By the time that it was 50 years old, its general condition was found to be deteriorating. In January 1915, Bowman Malcolm recommended to the Committee that it should be strengthened with new girders, but work was deferred until after the war. A report in August 1919 records that the bridge was in poor condition. Already, for some years the working timetables had contained a notice of a speed restriction on the bridge of 10 m.p.h., plus the information that 'the time taken to pass over the bridge should not be less than fifteen seconds. Double-headed trains not to be run over this bridge.' During the period of 'The Troubles' the management had more than enough civil engineering to cope with and the bridge work was again postponed. It was decided to rebuild it completely and a new girder structure replaced the old one; the work took from the beginning of April to the end of September 1924. On 13 September, Forbes issued the following 'Notice to the Travelling Public':

The Manager extremely regrets the inconvenience caused to Passengers for Derry in missing the Great Northern morning connections at Strabane, and the general forbearance of the public in this respect is very much appreciated.

It was obvious to those travelling between Stranorlar and Strabane that during the reconstruction and renewal of the large Girder Bridge over the Finn River near Clady, the trains had necessarily to be worked very cautiously and at restricted speeds (4 miles per hour). This working was slow, difficult and dangerous. The renewal was carried out by the Contractors—Messrs. Armstrong Whitworth & Co.—without stopping the traffic, and the work is now practically complete. It is therefore hoped that in about a week's time, trains will be able to run over the new bridge at normal speed, which will enable the general service to be speeded up, so that the usual connections can be made at Strabane with the Great Northern trains.

There, unfortunately, still continues to be some unavoidable delay to trains entering Donegal, due to the Customs regulations, but the travelling public are assured that special efforts are being made to minimise this, and as the Staff get more familiar with the requirements matters will improve.

THE RISE OF THE ROADS

It was only the poor state of the roads in County Donegal that throttled back competition from road vehicles. In other Irish counties where the roads were better, motor lorries and omnibuses came from cross-Channel factories and from army surplus sales in the early 1920s. The trickle developed within the next few years into a stream, as a multitude of back-yard owners, often backed by hire-purchase agreements, entered into a new and apparently profitable field of enterprise, offering the public a new form of wheeled transport, and at cut-throat prices. Competition was at first directed against the railways, statutorily incapable of entering into combat, and later lay between individual owners. It was exceptional for the privately-owned road vehicles to run in conjunction with the railways; rather than bring passengers to and from the stations at appropriate times, they preferred to compete over longer distances, even if unnecessary duplication of services resulted. Mutual reduction of fares brought the weaker road-men to their knees, and the railways had to make corresponding cuts in fares in an effort to win back patronage, at a time when rising operating costs should logically have been accompanied by fare increases.

In north Donegal, the Londonderry & Lough Swilly Company became road-omnibus owners in 1929, and thereafter systematically bought out various small firms who were operating against them. They were especially susceptible to road competition since their stations were in many cases several miles from the villages.

In south Donegal conditions tended to favour the railways, which linked village to village as efficiently as did the roads, and stations were better situated. But the advantages of having bus feeder-services were evident, and in September 1929 the Board asked Forbes to apply to the Ministry for Industry & Commerce in Dublin for approval of three projected bus routes: Glenties to Ardara, Glenties to Portnoo and Killybegs to Glencolumbkille. The Committee still lacked buses with which to work the proposed services and during the spring of 1930 Forbes made unsuccessful attempts to hire them. The Board then authorised him to buy four second-hand Reo buses at £270 for the four from the GNR, to pay the Irish Free State customs duty on them, and to start services.

These four buses lasted until 1933, by which time the Donegal roads had wrought such havoc on them that they were almost fit for scrap. Two were rebuilt into railcars. In 1933 four second-hand road lorries were bought and goods transport begun. The road lorry fleet rose to a total of 19 vehicles in 1936-7, fell to nine during the second war, and rose again to a total of 37 lorries and three tractors in 1957. In all the CDRJC bought 78 road freight vehicles between 1934 and 1959.

From 1933 until 1955 road omnibus services in the CDRJC's area were operated for the Committee by the GNR in concert with the rail services. Then, in 1955, the Joint Committee again took up the business of road passenger haulage, and their familiar black and white wall posters carried details of both rail and road services. By this time, as we shall see, the Glenties branch railway had been closed, and bus services were run on four routes: Stranorlar—Glenties—Portnoo, Glenties—Dungloe, Ballybofey—Letterkenny, and Malinmore—Killybegs. At Dungloe, in the district of the Rosses, the road services met those of the L & LS which had worked counter-clockwise from Londonderry round the north of Donegal.

RAILCARS REPLACE STEAM

In their attitude to road omnibus working, the CDRJC stood in contrast to the L & LS. The latter concern, once embarked on road bus workings, extended them rapidly, bought out competitors and eventually replaced all railway workings by an integrated bus and lorry service. On the other hand, Forbes and the Joint Committee, no doubt because they were fundamentally railwaymen and railway-directed, decided that they could best serve the public by modifying their rail services to suit local demands, that was, by stopping almost anywhere to pick up and set down.

The germ of this principle was to be seen in the little four-wheeled railcar which the CDRJC had bought in 1907. This vehicle, the same length as a city taxi and only standing six feet high, was originally powered by a 10 h.p. petrol engine and could carry ten people. It was used principally as a convenient service vehicle, and for conveying post office mails. Occasionally it was pressed into service for passengers. In 1914 the Board Minutes refer to its occasional use for additional mail conveyance: 'The small petrol rail motor, purchased six years ago for £237, would need to be overhauled, and this would cost around £50. If the Letterkenny night mails are to be carried for the G.P.O. for £600 per annum for seven-day service then we would need to buy a petrol rail motor at £600.' It appeared that the rail motor was lying in the Stranorlar shops, out of use and also apparently out of order.

Even if this original railcar, or 'rail motor' as it was termed, was used spasmodically, it had yielded valuable experience. In 1926, with the balance sheet insisting on lowered operating costs, Forbes decided that the time was ripe to show that his railway could give as flexible a service as the road omnibuses, and a faster one withal. It so happened that the Derwent Valley Light Railway, working south-eastwards from York, was ending passenger services and had a pair of Ford petrol-engined railcars for disposal. Forbes bought them for less than a quarter of what they had cost the DVLR a couple of years before, regauged them from 4 ft 8½ in. and lowered the bodies to match the level of the Donegal platforms. On the DVLR they had run in tandem, coupled back to back, but on the Donegal lines they were run separately. From the start they operated regular passenger services: by modern standards they were noisy and subjected the passengers to considerable vibration, but their ability to stop anywhere was deservedly popular in a country of small farms and isolated cottages. Furthermore, the operating costs were only a fraction of those of orthodox steam trains: in 1927 steam trains cost 11¼d per mile to run, the railcars 3¼d per mile. Admittedly, with steam trains the cost per seat-mile was lower, but on many of the services the 17 seats of the DVLR cars were sufficient.

After two years' experience a fourth petrol-driven railcar joined the fleet, and further additions brought the total to six by 1930. In the following year the first diesel-engined passenger-carrying vehicle on the railways of Britain went into service.

Petrol-engined railcars continued in use up until 1947, and were joined by an increasing number of diesel-engined vehicles. The seating capacity of the early railcars was limited by the wheelbase, but it was soon found that they had enough reserve of power to haul one or more light trailers. O'Doherty, the Strabane coach-builder, turned out the first of these, a 29-seater, in 1929. Later four trailers, seating 125 persons, were numbered in the fleet.

By 1940, 13 railcars and one trailer were at work, together able to carry 478 passengers. The maximum seating capacity the fleet reached was 508, in 1941-3, when 14 railcars and one trailer were employed. Then came withdrawals of the older cars, particularly in 1949, and the fleet shrank, though two new railcars were acquired in 1950 and 1951.

Until 1926 the annual Statistical Returns classed the original railcar as a service vehicle and any passenger mileage it ran was not separately recorded. Once it was joined by the two Derwent Valley railcars and the policy of railcar operating became established, the three were officially grouped together as passenger-carrying 'rail motor vehicles'. In 1926, that first, though incomplete, year of railcar working, their mileage was 7,480. This compared with 286,361 miles run by steam locomotives. Over the next seven years the steam total fell by around one-third, while railcars increased by leaps and bounds. In 1933 the two totals were practically the same, and in 1934 the railcars had drawn ahead, having run just over a quarter of a million miles compared to steam's 190,000.

The highest railcar mileage was in 1938 when the 13 vehicles ran up 313,508 miles. Oil and petrol rationing during World War II clipped the railcar running to about two-thirds of that, but without any significant compensatory increase in steam mileage.

There is no doubt that the policy which Forbes initiated, whereby railcars took over the bulk of the passenger haulage, was sound. Had the Committee adhered exclusively to steam haulage it is doubtful if the system could have survived until the outbreak of war. The bustling railcars, able to accelerate rapidly from the multitudinous stops, were treated as road buses would have been and they were popular with the people of Donegal. They were often worked by a single man, though a guard was usually carried. The crew's job was no sinecure; a constant watch had to be kept for passengers standing by the lineside, or huddled against a hedge out of the winter storms, the folding door had to be pulled open for them, and their tickets had to be issued if they had joined at an intermediate stop. Parcels had to be collected or set down, and 'as an obligement' many a bottle of medicine was handed out through a railcar window or an urgent message called to the nearest neighbour down the line.

The Committee were fortunate in having an obliging and friendly staff, but credit must be given to Forbes's painstaking instructions. Every copy of the working timetable and the bulkier red-bound appendix carried the message: 'REMEMBER! It is well for each Member of this organization to bear in mind that goodwill based upon years of conscientious effort may be entirely destroyed by a moment's carelessness or indifference toward a customer.'

For the railcar crews, inevitably brought into close contact with the passengers, Forbes issued a six-page book in 1934. Titled *Special Instructions to Railcar Drivers*, its contents were couched in plain, direct terms. It was typical of Forbes that its two sections, headed 'Your Passengers' and 'Your Car', came in that order. The first paragraph shows how much attention was bestowed on obtaining good relations between passengers and railcar crews:

'Be COURTEOUS to all, and do not be nervous of saying "please" and "thank you" even to the humblest. Be HELPFUL to all, particularly the aged or infirm, and give the same attention to those who find it difficult to pay their fare, as to the person with the suit case. Wear a smile, and show everybody that you are glad to see them using the railway. A satisfied customer is always the best advertisement.'

The good relations between the officers and staff were seen

during the 1933 railway strike when on the GNR there were two bad accidents caused by malicious interference with the track. Most of the Donegal railwaymen remained at work. Because of the effects of the general trade depression, which persisted up to the start of World War II, the men's wages were reduced by 10 per cent.

The original three classes of passenger accommodation, started by both the FVR and the WDR, continued up to the end of 1921. Second-class travel was then discontinued and the seating, which then represented 11 per cent of the total, was reallocated to the thirds. With the increase in one-class railcar working, first-class travel became something of an anomaly and it was ended from 1 January 1937. At that time, the CDRJC and the S & L together possessed 44 carriages seating 206 first and 1,573 third-class passengers. The conversion to a single class increased the seating capacity sufficiently to compensate for the scrapping of three old carriages in 1938.

DECLINE SETS IN

As the railcar fleet grew, the steam-locomotive stock was reduced. The six Neilson 4—6—0 tanks, bought by the DR in 1893, passed from the scene between 1931 and 1937. They were accompanied by the two 4—4—4 tanks in 1933, leaving, with one exception, a stock of engines that was entirely superheated. The carriage and wagon stock, however, changed little.

The annual net receipts, which had shown a profit since 1926, assumed a steep downward trend in 1930, and in 1931 they amounted to only £53. The next three years showed a loss in working, but recovery came in 1935 largely through an increase in third-class passenger traffic, and until 1940 a small profit was made on each year. It was clear, however, that the profit hung by a thread, and the system could only continue to exist by increased economies.

Many stories concern this time and Forbes's genius for improvisation and adaption. Instructions came from him that old, leaking vacuum bags were to be returned to stores and on more than one occasion he superintended the feeding of them on to a bonfire of scrap timber, on the waste ground by the sheds. When the red-hot wire spirals had fallen away from the burned rubber hose, they were caught with pliers and pulled out straight, coiled, and handed to the milesmen to be used in repairing the fences. Even if the savings were small, the bonfires demonstrated a principle.

The following figures show how during the thirties the costs of steam-locomotive working fell by around 50 per cent, but as this

Page 89: RAILCARS—3

(above) Railcar No. 9, at Stranorlar; (centre) Railcar No. 18, at Ballyshannon; (below) Trailer No. 2 ex-C & VBT

Page 90: DONEGAL STEAM

*(above) 'Erne' No. 14 halts from shunting in a picturesque setting:
(below) 'Blanche' No. 2 on a Stranorlar-Killybegs goods, east of Inver
station. Two coaches are in the train, for working back with a
special, July 1952*

was accompanied by an approximately similar drop in mileage, the cost per engine mile was about the same. The careful housekeeping that Forbes enforced during this period became a legend at Stranorlar, and the principle of make-do and mend was applied wherever considerations of safety permitted.

	Loco. working expenses	Cost per engine mile	Railcar working expenses	†Gross receipts	†Expenditure
1930	£14,170	11.1d	£418	£53,101	£47,395
1931	£12,909	10.8d	£568	£49,660	£46,347
1932	£11,576	10.6d	£1,156	£42,717	£44,312
1933	£8,443	10.6d	£1,837	£32,969	£36,784
1934	£8,430	10.7d	£2,309	£37,115	£40,384
1935	£7,387	10.3d	£2,612	£39,483	£37,285
1936	£6,813	10.3d	£2,636	£42,320	£34,790
1937	£7,009	11.4d	£2,462	£41,330	£35,812
1938	£6,853	11.5d	£2,530	£43,929	£34,790
1939	£7,493	13.0d	£2,273	£47,329	£34,763

† On railway working only.

There was also the home-made, weed-killing spray train. This was produced by the Stranorlar fitters from scrap wagons. A crank-driven pump, worked from the axle, drew sodium chlorate solution from three 40-gallon barrels and delivered it via a line of nozzles to the weeds. A truck behind carried three more barrels. In use, the contraption was towed behind No. 1 railcar and used to head out on its lethal duty at 5 a.m., putting a barrel of solution on every mile of ballast. Its cost was probably never calculated but it cannot have been high and it helped to ensure the track was kept clean, even though the milesmen's stretches had been lengthened. Discussing the spray unit's work with his permanent-way inspector after a successful season, Forbes's dry remark was 'I hope that the results will justify the expenditure'.

Once launched on his pursuit of economy, Forbes took a certain grim delight in getting full value for money. As a former Great Northern man he turned to that company for mechanical matters and found the great Dundalk works a prolific source of second-hand material—rails, road vehicles and diesel engines—to be bargained for and bought for his railway as cheaply as he could persuade the

COUNTY DONEGAL RAILWAYS.

SUNDAY SERVICES

GLENTIES — PORTNOC
ROSSNOWLAGH — KILLYBEGS.

Commencing SUNDAY 28th MAY 1939, and EACH SUNDAY until further notice, the following afternoon and evening services will run. Stops will be made anywhere to pick up or set down.—

STRABANE	dep.		p.m.	p.m.	p.m.	p.m.
CASTLEFIN			1. 5			
STRANORLAR	arr		1.20			
STRANORLAR	dep.		1.30			
FINTOWN				1.32	9.50	
GLENTIES	arr			2.25	10.35	
STRANORLAR	dep.		1.10	1.42		
DONEGAL	arr		1.55	2.25		
DONEGAL	dep.				2.30	9. 0
INVER					3. 0	9.30
KILLYBEGS	arr				3.30	10. 0
DONEGAL	dep.		2. 0	2.30		
ROSSNOWLAGH	arr		2.30	3. 0		
BALLYSHANNON	arr		2.45	3.15		

BALLYSHANNON	dep		p.m.	p.m.	p.m.
ROSSNOWLAGH					8.10
DONEGAL	arr				8.25
KILLYBEGS	dep.		1.20	7.50	8.55
INVER			1.50	8.20	
DONEGAL	arr		2.20	8.50	
DONEGAL	dep				9. 0
STRANORLAR	arr				9.15
GLENTIES	dep.		12.30	8.45	
FINTOWN			12.50	9. 5	
STRANORLAR			1.35	9.45	
STRANORLAR	dep				9.48
CASTLEFIN	arr				10. 8
STRABANE					10.23

Bicycles of passengers stored free at Stations at Owner's Risk.

The Services to and from Glenties are run in connection with G.N.R. buses between Glenties and Portnoo commencing SUNDAY, 25th JUNE. Bus leaves Glenties Station for Portnoo at 2.35 p.m. (on arrival of train) and return from Portnoo at 8.10 p.m. connecting with train at 8.45 p.m. Accommodation reserved in 'buses for rail-borne passengers. (See special handbill.)

CHEAP RETURN TICKETS (valid day of issue) :—

	Donegal and Rossmorlagh	Bally- shannon	Killy- begs	Glen- ties
STRABANE to KILLYGORDON inclusive	2 6	3 0	3 0	2 6
CAVAN and STRANORLAR	2 0	2 6	2 6	2 0
GLENTIES LINE STATIONS	2 6	3 0	3 0	—
GLENMORE and CLOGHAN	--	--	--	1 6
KILLYBEGS LINE STATIONS	2 0	2 6	--	--

Between other Stations usual cheap fares.

RAIL CARS STOP ANYWHERE ON REQUEST.

Stranorlar, 10th May, 1939.   Henry Forbes, Manager

Wall poster, 18″ x 23″, printed in black on yellow, advertising
Sunday services in the summer of 1939

not-so-rich uncle to part with them.

Peter Whitelaw, who had been the audit clerk at the time of the formation of the Joint Committee, had succeeded John Shields as accountant in 1925. Thirteen years later, Whitelaw retired and his place was taken at Stranorlar by Bernard L. Curran, who had been on the accountant's staff of the Northern Counties Committee at Belfast. Under Forbes and Curran, the system completed the last uneasy year of peace in Europe.

IMPACT OF WAR

The advent of World War II in 1939 dramatically altered the financial complexion of the CDRJC for a spell. Unlike the position in 1914-18, the bulk of the system's mileage and its administrative headquarters were in a neutral country. As a result it did not fall in any way under Government direction and did not participate in troop movements. Although Derry was an extremely important naval base, through which came vast quantities of military stores, this was practically without effect on the Joint Committee's line. War material in transit from Derry to other parts of Northern Ireland could not be routed over the Great Northern's Derry— Strabane line since it would have passed through seven miles of neutral Eire on the way. Use of the alternative narrow-gauge line, though entirely in Northern Ireland, was impractical for freight by reason of inadequate transhipment facilities at Strabane and so the bulk of the traffic was routed out of Derry over the broad-gauge NCC line towards Coleraine. The laying of a third rail, to give direct connection from the NCC station at Derry Waterside to Strabane, was seriously considered then, but was not carried out.

Diesel railcar operation and road freight services were so far advanced by the outbreak of war that certain economies in buildings were possible. Two goods stores became redundant and were demolished, at Laghey in 1939 and at Rossnowlagh in 1943. The Ballyshannon branch carried a light traffic except for occasional excursions, and as it was adequately served by a railcar, the carriage shed was taken down in 1942. Around this time various small pieces of surplus land were sold.

From 1940 until 1945, although working in a country not at war, the financial results of the CDRJC exhibited trends common with the systems across the border. The total wages bill of enginemen and motormen increased by between 45 per cent and 50 per cent, coal costs rose by 109 per cent and fuel oil by 80 per cent. The

Rail-Car Stopping Places

On and from Tuesday, 1st August, 1944, Rail-Cars will only stop at Stations, Halts (with the exception of Town Bridge, Hospital Halt and Glassagh Halt), and the undernoted special Stopping Places.

The travelling public are respectfully urged to co-operate with the Company in this matter, which is necessary owing to Fuel Oil restrictions, difficulty in securing Rail-Car parts, and to enable the services to be run at the times scheduled in the Company's Time-tables.

FINN VALLEY SECTION

County Home Gate

WEST DONEGAL SECTION

Quinn's Crossing,
Lough Gates,
Dunnion's Crossing,
Townawilly Crossing,
Harvey's Hill

KILLYBEGS SECTION

Drimark Hill,
No. 18 Gates
No 20 Gates (Bettles)
Spamount
No. 30 Gates

BALLYSHANNON SECTION

Drumbar
No 41 Gates
Dromore
Dorrian s Bridge,
McCann's Crossing,
Kildoney Crossing

GLENTIES SECTION

Gallinagh's Gates
Ballindoon Bridge
Double Gates
Cronadun Bridge
No 36 Gates (S. Doherty's)
Ballast Pit,
Brennan s Gates
No 38 Gates (McMonagle s)

LETTERKENNY SECTION

No 53 Gates (Linney s)
Killen s Gate Signal
No 62 Gates (Baird's)

Passengers joining or alighting from vehicles at stopping places other than Stations or Halts do so at their own risk

Steam Trains will only stop at Stations and Halts

Stranorlar
24/7/'44

B L CURRAN,
Acting Manager

Handbill issued in July 1944 listing 'official' stopping places for railcars. These stopping places had grown so numerous over the 18 years of railcar operation that it had become difficult to maintain timetable schedules, and the number of stops was officially reduced as listed above

number of passenger journeys practically doubled its pre-war total, rising to 522,000 in 1945. An increase in the average fare per passenger journey from 9.6d to 12.0d brought the passenger receipts up to almost £26,000 in 1945, compared to £11,000 in 1940. Livestock movements varied fairly widely from year to year, but in general they were doubled, as fewer cattle entered Britain from abroad. The pattern of increased expenditure, increased revenue and increased profits reflected, in a smaller way, the experience of the Joint Committee's parent companies.

CURRAN FOLLOWS FORBES

Then, on 7 November 1943, close by the railway that for 30 years had been his life, Henry Forbes died suddenly in his home at Stranorlar. There thus passed from the Irish railway scene one of its most forceful and colourful personalities. A strict disciplinarian and perhaps regarded with fear rather than with affection by some of his men, he was yet able to inspire them to an unmatched standard of competence and courtesy. The undertaking suffered a severe loss by his death, but it was fortunate that the gap that was left was so ably filled by B. L. Curran, who by then had spent five years under Forbes's tutelage.

While paying due tribute to the remarkable personality of Henry Forbes, it would perhaps be wrong to regard his course of action as an absolutely successful one. In many respects he was a law unto himself. During his time at Stranorlar he fought with and virtually refused to recognise the Trades Unions. That such an attitude was tolerated as long as it was is a reflection both of the respect in which he was held by his employees and of the fact that Trades Unionism was not yet firmly entrenched among his workpeople. In many another place Forbes would have been forced into capitulation by strike action, but as it was, he got away with it. The attitude of his successor in office was, and in the circumstances had to be, very different, and Curran, gentler and more accommodating, was most meticulous in observing the letter of agreements.

While we may choose to marvel, or to be amused, at Forbes's endless pursuit of economy, taking a dispassionate view one is forced to conclude that it was an obsession and in the long run was responsible for the premature end of the railway. It must be remembered that after 1906 the system was not owned by a small company scraping along from year to year with limited revenue and with a wary eye on dividends. There were no shareholders, but instead two large owning companies to whom, until the middle thirties, the provision of a few thousands of pounds of capital was a mere bagatelle. But to the Committee, what Forbes said was gospel and the wisdom of his cheeseparing tactics was apparently never seriously questioned. Neither were many of his proposals on engineering matters, though occasionally Glover and later Howden were to challenge his more impractical schemes.

So it was that, during the twenties and thirties, neither permanent way nor rolling stock were systematically renewed, as they could easily have been with capital from the owning companies. Instead the condition of both steadily deteriorated. Then, in the middle of a world war, Curran was left to cope with a situation that could only be remedied by urgent and wholesale renewals. But for some years before the outbreak of war, the Great Northern themselves had been in financial difficulties, and as owners of one-half of the Donegal, they objected to any avoidable capital expenditure, whether overdue or not. The attitude of the LMS might have been more generous, but capital had to be provided in equal shares. Curran's task was neither easy nor enviable, and there were widespread shortages of raw materials. What was spent was reflected in working expenses.

FLOOD DAMAGE

On the afternoon of 10 September 1946 the north-west of Ireland was affected by very heavy rain and the rivers and streams rose in spate. A mile from Killybegs at milepost 49¼, where the railway was on an embankment over 30 ft in height, a stream ran down from the hills and entered the land-locked bay. The stream was taken through the embankment by a masonry culvert with an arched roof. The culvert was of ample size to carry the flood water, but one side-wall had been undercut by scour until it collapsed. The arched roof followed and, left without support the embankment slumped into the stream. Micky Lafferty, driving a railcar, passed at an early stage in the trouble and fortunately saw what was happening, and reported it. The line was at once closed to traffic.

Restoration of the line was too big a job to be undertaken by the CDRJC with their limited equipment and manpower. After an inspection by the civil engineer on 11 September, it was decided that the work should be done by Messrs McLaughlin and Harvey Ltd who were then carrying out a large contract for the Electricity Supply Board at Ballyshannon and had the necessary heavy plant reasonably near. They were assisted by the CDRJC platelayers.

The civil engineer's report to the Joint Committee, dated 18 September, estimated the cost of the repairs at £2,500 and the duration of the work at four weeks. Meanwhile, the branch beyond Donegal was completely closed, and a substitute bus and lorry service organised. In the event, the job dragged out far beyond the four weeks, and the line was not reopened until 19 February 1947. During that period of 22 weeks, locomotive No. 4 and a railcar— either No. 7 or No. 8, were locked up in Killybegs.

NEW SIDING FOR OLD

To get material urgently needed at the wash-out at milepost 49¼, 27 yds of surplus siding were taken out of the yard at Mountcharles. In compensation, as it were, for this loss, a new 400 ft siding was put in about the same time at Derg Bridge, at the eastern end of Barnesmore Gap. Here, moraine deposits of sand and gravel were heaped against the flanks of the mountain, and these provided ideal raw material for concrete work in connection with the Erne Barrage at Ballyshannon.

The new siding cost around £300 to lay in. Along it came nearly 20,000 tons of sand, which was railed to Ballyshannon station. Between the railway and the contractors, Cementation Ltd, a rate of 4s per ton for conveyance was agreed upon. It was the last occasion when the system carried any large tonnage of mineral traffic.

RETRENCHMENT

During the years of World War II, when the undertaking was making a profit, the Joint Committee prudently set aside a total of £34,150, which was placed in a Contingency Fund. This Fund was used to meet the losses incurred after 1948, and thereby reduced the amount which had to be made good by the two owners. By 1958, the Contingency Fund had been reduced to £1,190, and losses continued to mount.

Shortly after the end of the war in Europe, the removal of strict petrol rationing brought the travel-hungry private motorists back to the roads. On the Committee's lines, passenger journeys were well maintained until 1947, but then a marked and steady decrease set in. Fare increases were insufficient to balance the loss in income. To remain solvent, further economy in upkeep was required, and the necessary track work was postponed, though by this time the condition of the rolling stock and stations was far better than it had been ten years earlier.

Further retrenchment was to come. The income from the Glenties branch did not justify its being maintained and the last regular passenger and goods service ran on it on 13 December 1947. The line remained open for occasional trains carrying turf, livestock or bog iron ore. On 19 September 1949 the last train, a steam-hauled stock special with sheep, ran out as far as Cloghan, and the line lay derelict. On 10 March 1952 the branch was closed to all traffic and rails and bridges were sold to the Hammond Lane Metal Co. of Dublin. Lifting began in 1953 and in August 1955 the last sections of the Finn River bridge at Stranorlar were dismantled.

As economy measures to keep the line open, the goods store at Ballintra, the staff section midway down the Ballyshannon branch, was demolished in 1949, the E.T.S. instruments were removed in 1951 and the signal cabin was taken down in 1953.

With the fall in goods traffic, extensive scrapping of wagons took place in 1947, though some useful additions came from second-hand Clogher Valley stock and were used as railcar trailer wagons.

An unfortunate year was 1949, during which one of the railcars was wrecked and three persons in it were killed, in a head-on collision with a steam goods on the Ballyshannon branch close to Donegal. A second railcar was extensively damaged by fire at Sessiaghoneill, between Stranorlar and Barnesmore. Two more rail-cars then 18 years old and worn out, were scrapped.

The average age of the carriage stock was now over the half-century and a major programme of withdrawals and scrapping took place in 1950-2. In compensation two new railcars were purchased. From the closed Ballycastle branch of the Ulster Transport Authority came three noteworthy additions, massive corridor coaches that had been built in 1928 for the long-defunct boat trains between Ballymena and Larne.

From 10 August 1948, the Strabane—Londonderry branch had been a part of the rail system of the Ulster Transport Authority, as successor to the Northern Counties Committee. The branch continued to be worked by the Joint Committee. The UTA was in no mood to support uneconomic lines and because of the loss incurred it was decided to withdraw all services on this branch. Notice was given of this intention in October 1954 under the provisions of Section 57 of the Transport Act (Northern Ireland) 1948. Services ended on the last day of December 1954. The line came temporarily to life again on 30 June 1955 when a Sunday School excursion special was run, carrying 600 children *en route* from Strabane to Portrush. Then on 23 September 1955 the Minister of Commerce made an Order for the abandonment of this section of line and shortly afterwards the track was lifted. Victoria Road station was sold to a firm of wholesale grocers, who retained the starter signal at the platform end as witness of their premises' former glories, and kept it pulled 'off' when open. With the end of the Derry services the mileage of line worked by the CDRJC was reduced to 85½.

From January 1948 the share of the CDRJC formerly owned by the LMS passed, on nationalisation in Britain, to the Railway Executive (London Midland Region), and then in 1953 to the British Transport Commission (LM Region). These two bodies continued to appoint their three representatives to the Joint Committee.

The original stock of the DR had been exchanged for stock in the owning companies under the terms of the 1906 Act. By 1953 the British Transport Commission's share consisted of £318,345 of 3 per cent stock, which earned £9,550 interest each year. This interest was paid by the Joint Committee to the BTC, who passed it on to the holders of the Donegal Railway stock.

By 1953, operating losses had overtaken the other owner, the GNR, and that Company had come to the end of its resources. To maintain essential transport services the two Governments had acted in concert, and had assumed responsibility for the financial affairs of the Company. From 1 September 1953 the functions of the GNR had been taken over by the GNR Board, a statutory body constituted by two Acts, one passed by the Oireachtas of the Republic, and the other by the Parliament of Northern Ireland. The Great Northern's share of liability for interest in the CDRJC's affairs was thus assumed equally by the two Governments. Apart from interest, the GNR Board's share of the annual losses was borne by its two sponsors in the ratio of track mileage in the two countries.

From 1955 until 1958, operation of the CDRJC's lines followed the existing pattern, but with a general fall in traffic. It was noteworthy however that excursions continued to be well patronised. This was especially so in 1955 when in July and August bookings were very heavy. Eight special trains ran to Rossnowlagh with 4,488 passengers, and eight other excursion trains conveyed a total of 7,732 passengers. The wisdom of retaining a good stock of the elderly carriages was borne out, and the sight of double-headed steam workings up the banks leading to the Barnesmore Gap will be long remembered by those who saw them.

Container traffic, both for bread and for general merchandise, had been greatly developed by the GNR and to a lesser degree by Coras Iompair Eireann. On the Donegal, under GNR guidance, some wagons were adapted for this purpose in 1955, and the first runs were made with CIE containers routed between Dublin and Letterkenny. They could be customs-sealed, and their use reduced the journey time between the two places by 24 hours.

THE END OF THE RAILWAY

By 1957 it was evident, even to the most optimistic, that the days of the system were numbered. It appeared likely that the Ballyshannon branch would be the first to go, and the Joint Committee applied to the Transport Tribunal for an Order to permit its closure. They submitted that the estimated loss on the branch in 1956 was £3,435, and that it could be replaced by road services. The only objectors to the application were the Donegal County Council, who claimed that the tourist industry would suffer as a result of the loss of rail services, and that the existing roads were inadequate to carry the increased traffic. The decision of the Tribunal was that the branch should be closed as soon as the necessary road improvements had been made.

Pending the completion of the road repairs, the Ballyshannon branch was still open when, at the end of May 1959, the Joint Committee made formal application to end all railway services on the rest of their lines. Objections were to be submitted to the Transport Tribunal before 1 July. The necessary permission was granted, and all regular services were posted to come to an end on the last day of December 1959.

On the evening of 30 December 1959, the last of the Baltic tanks, *Erne*, now 54 years old, worked a long goods train up from Strabane. Ballyshannon was making sure of its coal supplies and received nine wagons, with nearly 20 covered wagons besides. With James McMenamin driving and his brother Francis firing to him, they left Stranorlar after the last railcar had slipped down from Donegal. They headed towards the Gap in pitch darkness, a soft, quiet night carrying the slowing exhaust beat as they took the bank towards Meenglas, the last goods train to work over the old West Donegal section.

On the last day of the old year, railcar No. 12 driven by Christie Kennedy was the last to work out of Killybegs. The mails had gone four hours earlier on board No. 16. Normally No. 12

would have gone on to Strabane after its Stranorlar call, but with visitors and Finn Valley folk the railcar would have been filled four times over. So its departure was held for 20 minutes, while the throng, delighted at the novelty, crowded into a special steam train driven by the McMenamins: *Drumboe* and five coaches. To Strabane and back they went, through darkness and drizzling rain, and over volleys of exploding detonators, and with their return to Stranorlar at 8.21 p.m. there ended the last passenger working on the County Donegal.

The County Donegal had gone down fighting. It was in complete accord with the traditions established by Henry Forbes that it should have done so, and that in its last days the system should not have sunk into disrepute or disuse. Up to the very end it served its public as well as they could have wished, and bearing in mind the changed economic conditions against which it laboured, its survival until then was a tribute to the energies of Forbes and Curran and the men that they worked with.

SEQUELAE

With the end of public rail services, on and from 1 January 1960, the public were offered substitute road services. For some, buses from CIE were painted in the Joint Committee's livery of red and cream and were operated over the following routes:

Strabane—Lifford—Ballybofey—Donegal
Donegal—Killybegs
Donegal—Ballyshannon
Strabane—Letterkenny via Raphoe
Strabane—Letterkenny via White Cross
Stranorlar—Glenties—Portnoo
Ballybofey—Stranorlar—Letterkenny
Malinmore—Glencolumbkille—Killybegs

The entry into Northern Ireland was necessarily over the half-mile of road linking Lifford with Strabane, where the Customs Posts were situated. At the Lifford end, this road crossed the River Foyle by a stone bridge a short way below the confluence of the Mourne and Finn Rivers. This bridge was due for renewal and was decided by the authorities to be unsafe for heavy road bus and lorry traffic. For a time passengers had to change buses and cross the bridge on foot. An Ulster Transport Authority bus conveyed them to and from the railway station at Strabane, but before travellers into Northern Ireland could reach the station they had to endure another stop for examination by the Northern Customs.

Replacement of the old bridge was a long-term matter in the hands of the Tyrone and Donegal County Councils, and to simplify the antics to which their patrons had been subjected, the Joint Committee took the matter into their own hands. They possessed a perfectly good bridge of their own, carrying the disused track of the s & l a quarter of a mile down river from the road bridge. As speedily as possible, the track was lifted between Strabane and Lifford and a private roadway laid in its place. The work was begun on New Year's Day 1960 and was finished on 25 January. Thereafter the CDRJC buses and lorries were able to run to and from Strabane station.

During this period an interim goods-train service was worked up the Finn Valley section. The oldest section of the system was thus the last to go. Three trains per day were run in each direction, two by railcar and one by steam. The first steam working, on New Year's Day 1960, was by *Meenglas*, hauling a train of five wagons and a third-brake carriage No. 23, and driven by Inspector McBride with J. McKenna firing. The regular workings ended on 6 February 1960, though an occasional train ran after that. While the service lasted, customs examination was done at Castlefinn and at Strabane, and the Clady frontier post was closed.

The immediate lifting of the line between Strabane and Lifford was followed soon afterwards by a breach of the line close to Ballyshannon as a result of road improvements. The Lifford breach resulted in the line out to Letterkenny being isolated from the rest of the system, and with it the 4—6—4 tank engine *Erne* which was lying at Letterkenny.

The melancholy task of lifting the track on the rest of the system started at the end of March 1960 at Ballyshannon. Motive power for the demolition work consisted of railcars 18 and 12, coupled back to back. No. 18 was then damaged, and was brought back to Stranorlar and replaced by No. 16. No. 12 railcar remained on the branch, but each evening the other railcar returned to Stranorlar. The work was finished by mid-June, and the two railcars were transferred to the Killybegs line. By mid-August the track had been lifted into Inver, and to Donegal by 8 September. The rails were stacked for removal by road transport, at various points along the system.

. Starting on 4 July, the old West Donegal section was lifted, using steam locomotive No. 4 and a motor-driven haulage wagon which tore the rails clear of the sleepers. By early August Barnesmore Gap was devoid of rails and the task was complete in five weeks.

The old s & l line was attacked from two ends. The road was broken between Coolaghy and Raphoe, near milepost 5, and was lifted into Letterkenny by the end of August, using *Erne*. The remainder was dealt with by *Phoenix* working in from Lifford.

Last to be demolished was the Finn Valley section, where motive power was provided by *Meenglas* and railcar No. 10.

The removal of the railway left the motive power scattered. Stranorlar shed housed *Alice*, *Lydia* and *Columbkille*. *Blanche*, *Meenglas* and *Drumboe* were at Strabane and *Erne* had dug in at Letterkenny. The lifting of the West Donegal section had left railcars 12 and 16 at Donegal. Railcar 10 lay at Strabane, whilst the remaining five railcars (Nos. 14, 15, 18, 19 and 20) were at Stranorlar.

Fortunately, during the year the future of the Belfast Transport Museum had become assured and larger premises had replaced the cramped motor-shed of the former Belfast & County Down Railway. As a result, the Museum acquired the steam locomotive *Blanche*, the diesel-tractor *Phoenix*, the ex-Clogher Valley railcar No. 10 and the ex-Dublin & Blessington trailer No. 3.

If the Donegal had followed the course of its predecessors (with the exception of the Cavan & Leitrim) the rest of its stock would have gone for scrap. Before this could happen, Dr Ralph Cox of Wildwood, New Jersey, became interested in it and made two purchases with a view to setting up a small private railway in the U.S.A. His first purchase comprised the steam locomotives *Meenglas* and *Drumboe*, railcar No. 18, 10 coaches, 20 covered wagons, 20 wagon chassis, 100 tons of rails and fastenings, 10 tons of points and signal rodding, and the Stranorlar signal cabin and turntable. He followed this up with a second purchase during the formal public auction on 1 March 1961, and became the owner of loco-motives *Erne* and *Columbkille*, railcars Nos. 12 and 16, 14 wagon chassis, an 18-ft turntable and the verandah roof from Stranorlar station.

The public auction saw the disposal of *Alice* and *Lydia* for scrapping, together with railcars 14 and 15. The newest pair of railcars, 19 and 20, were bought by the Isle of Man Railway. The total sum realised by the sale amounted to around £8,000.

The American purchase ended in anti-climax. Seven years later, all the material, neatly assembled at Strabane, Stranorlar and Letter-kenny for shipment, was still awaiting the boat that never docked at Derry. The shipping bill was estimated to run into five figures sterling. At Stranorlar, some of Dr Cox's purchases were under the surveillance of the headquarters offices, or under cover, and they remained intact. But at Letterkenny, *Erne* lay in the open, as did *Meenglas* and *Drumboe* at Strabane. For some years the Great Northern continued to work into Derry until they too followed the Donegal into oblivion, and their line was lifted. By 1966 Strabane station, that fascinating blend of gauges and colours, lay derelict and open to vandals. By then, the once-gleaming red and cream paint on the carriages was flaking and dull, although the sixty-year-old plate glass in the windows was keeping out the weather as well as ever. Within another year, smashed windows and shattered timber work proclaimed the work of the village idiots, while the two engines had lost all that could be torn off them. It was a sad end to it all.

CHAPTER VI

Working the System

TRAIN SERVICES AND OPERATING

Although the Finn Valley Minute Books do not contain full details of the train services, one can gain from them the information that three trains ran in each direction on weekdays in 1863. There were no Sunday workings.

The earliest timetable that the writer has seen is dated 1874, and shows the same scheme of working as at the start. The 'up' trains left Stranorlar at 8 a.m., 1 p.m. and 8 p.m. With only minor alterations in timing, this service continued into the days of the DR company. Calls were always made at the intermediate stations, Killygordon, Liscooly, Castlefinn and Clady, and the running time varied from 42 to 55 minutes.

By the turn of the century, the service had increased to five trains, which left in the up direction at 5.10 a.m., 8.10 a.m., 10.31 a.m., 4 p.m. and 5.20 p.m. A sixth train was added in the following summer. Sometime about 1910 and until the outbreak of war, a seventh train ran on Tuesdays: thus in June 1913 the departures from Strabane were 5.5 a.m. mail, which ran through to Killybegs, 8 a.m. Ballyshannon train, 10.33 a.m. to Stranorlar with connections to Glenties and Killybegs, 1.30 p.m. on Tuesdays and Strabane Fair days only, 3.55 p.m. through train to Glenties, 5.28 p.m. through train to Killybegs, and finally the 9 p.m. goods to Stranorlar which had 3rd class passenger accommodation. Workings from Stranorlar left at 9.5 a.m., 11.15 a.m., 11.45 a.m. goods and 3rd class, 2.25 p.m., 4.45 p.m. and 7.42 p.m., while a light engine at 3 p.m. on Tuesdays and Strabane Fair days balanced the down passenger working mentioned.

There does not appear to have been any regular Sunday services over the Finn Valley section until the summer of 1912. By then, under Forbes' management, the appeal of the seaside had been publicised, and from 8 June to 28 September a train left Strabane at 8.30 a.m. and arrived at Ballyshannon 2 hours 25 minutes later.

It returned from Ballyshannon at 5.45 p.m. The next year, it was possible to make the journey from Derry, with a change at Strabane. By 1916, it had become a through working from Derry, leaving at 7.45 a.m. and return the sun-weary families at 8.51 p.m. In 1917, the Sunday trains were withdrawn and were never reinstated.

Over the Finn Valley section, and elsewhere, steam-hauled passenger trains were often mixed, and steam goods trains were run as desired. In addition, coal specials were allotted paths and were run when required. Four such are shown in the 1912 working timetable; the trains conveyed coal to Stranorlar from the port of Derry:

Coal Special No. 1 (empty wagons)	Stranorlar	7.55 a.m.	Derry	9.30 a.m.
„ „ No. 2 (full wagons)	Derry	11.00 a.m.	Stranorlar	1.00 p.m.
„ „ No. 3 (empty wagons)	Stranorlar	3.10 p.m.	Derry	4.35 p.m.
„ „ No. 4 (full wagons)	Derry	5.30 p.m.	Stranorlar	7.20 p.m.

On the West Donegal Railway, out to the terminus at Druminin, the early trains mirrored those on the FVR section: the 1889 time-table shows departures from Stranorlar at 8.20 a.m., 12.20 p.m. and 6.15 p.m., with the journey taking 40 minutes. From Druminin, trains left at 7.20 a.m., 11.20 a.m. and 7 p.m.; it is unlikely that an engine lay overnight at Druminin to work the early up train, so that either an earlier empty carriage, light engine or else a mail/goods working was probably needed.

Before the first war, there were four trains each way between Stranorlar and Donegal, winter and summer. In 1911, first away was the 5.45 a.m. (the Mail ex-Strabane), then the 9.5 a.m., 11.13 a.m. after which a seven-hour gap intervened until the 6.10 p.m. left. With the exception of the second train, all went through to Killybegs. A similar service lasted through the war, but in 1919 the service was reduced to two trains each way. By 1921 a third train had been restored, though it was not until 1930 that four trains reappeared in the timetable. Railcars then began to improve matters, and by 1936 we find that no less than six services ran, with the down trains timed to leave Stranorlar at 8.35 a.m., 11.05 a.m., 2.10 p.m., 3.40 p.m., 5.55 p.m. and 6.45 p.m., five of these going on to Killybegs Generally, in these latter years, there were four winter and six summer workings in each direction.

Donegal-Killybegs traffic was less heavy than on either of the foregoing sections of the system, and at first the usual three trains sufficed. In the summer of 1900, these left Donegal at 7 a.m., 12.10 p.m. and 7.10 p.m., and Killybegs at 6.45 a.m., midday and 5.10 p.m.

Page 107 : COACHING STOCK—1

(above) Trailer No. 13, ex-D & BST; (centre) Carriage No. 1, ex-WDR, at Stranorlar in 1959; (below) Carriage No. 29, with original end verandahs and DR livery

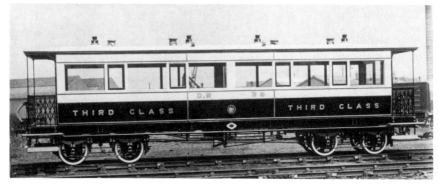

Page 108: COACHING STOCK—2

(above) Lavatory composite (1st/2nd) No. 37; (centre) Corridor 3rd No. 39, with original end verandahs; (below) 3rd class luggage van No. 42

The run took 75 minutes and stops were made at Killymard, Mount-charles, Doorin Road, Inver, Port, Dunkineely, Bruckless and Ardara Road. All the trains were through workings to and from Stranorlar. In the summer of 1910, there was a Sunday run which arrived at Killybegs at 11.25 a.m. and returned at 5.15 p.m. It was comparable to the Sunday train to Ballyshannon already referred to, but it must have been less popular, for by 1912 it had been dropped.

Over the Glenties line, three steam trains and later three railcar services provided an adequate timetable. In the down direction in 1911, the mails went up the valley on the 5.52 a.m. ex-Stranorlar. This train returned at 7.30 a.m. The midday train left Stranorlar at 11.25 a.m., arrived in Glenties at 12.45 p.m., and left for Stranorlar at 1.5 p.m. The third pair of workings were the 4.40 p.m. ex-Stranorlar and the 6.20 p.m. ex-Glenties. Down trains were timed at 80 minutes, up trains could clip this to 66 minutes.

At the start, the Ballyshannon branch had the familiar three trains up and down. With motive power based at the small Ballyshannon shed, first train of the day in the summer of 1906 left at 9.15 a.m. and was into Donegal in 50 minutes. The last train left Donegal at 7.20 p.m. Traffic seems to have been disappointing, for on 24 March 1909 it was minuted that the Committee had decided to cut the branch service to two trains per day, with three on Saturdays only. Local criticism resulted in a restoration of the cuts in 1910. The through workings on Sundays from Strabane and Derry between 1912 and 1917 have been referred to above. After their withdrawal, they were not restored until 1940.

The Ballyshannon branch provided an ideal line for Forbes' railcars, and their use enabled the daily service to be increased to four and later to five runs each way. Extra runs were made from Ballyshannon to Rossknowlagh during the summer, and a regular feature was a train for church-goers between these place on Sunday mornings.

The Strabane-Derry road, worked for the NCC, had always a better service than other parts of the system, as befitted a line that had one end in a city. The service at the 1900 opening showed six trains up and down: leaving Derry at 7.15 and 9.45 a.m., and 12.5, 3.10, 4.25 and 7.25 p.m., and leaving Strabane at 8.30 and 9.50 a.m., and at 12.10, 3.15, 6.00 and 8.30 p.m. The run occupied from 40 to 47 minutes, with Donemana as the crossing place.

A Sunday train was introduced over the Derry road in 1912. It left Strabane at 9 a.m. while the return run did not leave Derry until 7 p.m. It was this return working that was involved in the

WORKING TIME TABLE on and from 1st MAY, 1921.

DOWN TRAINS.—Week Days.

Distance from Strabane.		STATIONS.		1	2	3	4 Donegal Fair Days only. Goods only.	5 Goods and Passengers.	6	7 Donegal Fair Days only. Goods only.	8	9
				a.m.	a.m.	a.m.	a.m.	p.m.	p.m.	p.m.	p.m.	p.m.
14¼	MIDLAND RY. N.C.C.	Derry (V.R.)	dep.	..	..	6 50	..	..	2 0	..	..	4 25
11¾		New Buildings	,,	..	..	6 59	..	..	2 9	..	..	4 34
9½		Desertone Halt	,,	..	..	—	..	..	*	..	..	*
8¼		Cullion	,,	..	..	7 10	..	..	2 25	..	..	4 45
6¼		Donemana	,,	..	..	7 18	..	..	2 40	..	..	4 53
4½		B'heather Halt	,,	..	..	—	..	..	*	..	..	—
2¾		Ballymagorry	,,	..	..	7 31	..	..	3 0	..	..	5 6
		Strabane	arr.	..	..	7 40	..	..	3 10	..	..	5 15
		Strabane	dep.	..	..	7 55	..	2 0	3 15	4 0	..	5 25
4½		Clady	,,	..	..	8 5	..	*	3 27	*	..	5 37
6¼		Castlefinn	,,	..	..	8 12	..	*	3 33	*	..	5 44
8¼		Liscooly	,,	..	..	*	..	*	3 39	*	..	*
9¾		Killygordon	,,	..	..	8 30	..	*	3 46	*	..	5 54
13¾		Stranorlar	arr.	..	..	8 40	..	3 0	3 55	4 37	..	6 4
	BRANCH.	Stranorlar	dep.	LINE CLOSED on and from 15th April, 1921.	..	↓	..	..	↓	..	..	..
14¼		Ballybofey	,,		..		..	..		..	..	..
17¾		Glenmore	,,		..		..	..		..	..	..
20½		Cloghan	,,		..		..	..		..	..	..
27		Ballinamore	,,		..		..	..		..	..	..
29¾		Fintown	,,		..		..	..		..	..	..
34¾		Shallogans Halt	,,		..		..	..		..	..	..
38¼		Glenties	arr.		..	Y	..	..	Y	..	..	..
		Stranorlar	dep.	..	..	8 47	10 45	..	3 58	..	..	..
16½		Meen Glas Halt	,,	..	..	—	—	..	—	..	..	..
21½		Derg Bridge Halt	,,	..	..	*	—	..	*	..	..	..
25½		Barnesmore Halt	,,	..	..	—	—	..	*	..	..	..
27½		Lough Eske	,,	..	..	9 35	11 35	..	4 38	..	..	..
29½		Clar Bridge Halt	,,	..	..	*	—	..	*	..	..	..
31½		Donegal	arr.	..	..	9 48	11 45	..	4 50	..	..	..
	BRANCH.	Donegal	dep.	10 15	..	↓	..	..	↓	..	5 10	..
33		Drumbar Halt	,,	—	..		..	..		..	—	..
34¾		Laghey	,,	10 25	..		..	..		..	5 20	..
36½		Bridgetown	,,	*	..		..	..		..	*	..
38½		Ballintra	,,	10 38	..		..	..		..	5 35	..
41¾		Rossnowlagh	,,	10 50	..		..	..		..	5 45	..
43		Creevy Halt	,,	*	..		..	..		..	*	..
47		Ballyshannon	arr	11 5	..	Y	..	..	Y	..	6 0	..
		Donegal	dep.	..	..	10 0	..	..	5 0	..	..	..
34¼		Killymard Halt	,,	..	..	—	..	..	—	..	..	..
35¾		Mountcharles	,,	..	..	10 20	..	..	5 20	..	..	..
37½		Doorin Road	,,	..	..	10 27	..	..	5 27	..	..	..
39¾		Inver	,,	..	..	10 35	..	..	5 35	..	..	..
41½		Port Halt	,,	..	..	*	..	..	—	..	..	..
43¾		Dunkineely	,,	..	..	10 55	..	..	5 50	..	..	..
46		Bruckless	,,	..	..	11 3	..	..	5 58	..	..	..
48¼		Ardara Road	,,	..	..	*	..	..	*	..	..	..
50½		Killybegs	arr.	..	..	11 20	..	..	6 15	..	..	..

CROSSING ARRANGEMENTS.

No. 6 Train to cross No 19 at Derry and No. 27 at Donegal.
No. 9 Train to cross No. 24 at Derry and No. 27 at Stranorlar.
No. 3 Train to cross No. 18 at Lough Eske.
No. 5 Train to cross No. 24 Train at Castlefin (Donegal Fair Day).

* Will call to pick up or set down Passengers if required. Guard to keep a sharp look-out approaching.

☞ **The times allowed for the running of the trains on the Strabane and Derry Section must not, under any circumstances, be reduced.**

UP TRAINS.—Week Days.

Distance from Strabane.	STATIONS.		14	15	16	17	18	19	24	25	26	27
								Goods and Passengers to Strabane. Goods ONLY to Derry.	Donegal Fair Days only. Donegal to Strabane.			
			a.m.	a.m.	a.m.	a.m.	a.m.	a.m.	p.m.	p.m.	p.m.	p.m.
50½	**Killybegs**	dep.	..	..	..	..	8 0	..	..	..	..	3 30
48¼	Ardara Road	,,	..	..	..	..	*	..	..	..	..	*
46	Bruckless	,,	..	..	..	..	8 15	..	..	..	..	3 45
43¾	Dunkineely	,,	..	..	..	..	8 25	..	..	..	..	3 57
41½	Port Halt	,,	..	..	..	..	*	..	..	..	..	*
39¾	**Inver**	,,	..	..	..	..	8 38	..	..	..	..	4 15
37¼	Doorin Road	,,	..	..	..	..	8 45	..	..	..	..	4 23
35¾	Mountcharles	,,	..	..	..	..	8 55	..	..	..	..	4 32
34¼	Killymard Halt	,,	..	..	..	..	—	..	..	..	..	—
31½	**Donegal**	arr.	..	..	..	..	9 10	..	..	..	..	4 49
	BRANCH.											
47	**Ballyshannon**	dep	..	..	..	8 20	|	..	..	3 50	..	|
43	Creevy Halt	,,	..	..	..	*	|	..	..	*	..	|
41¾	Rossnowlagh	,,	..	..	..	8 35	|	..	..	4 5	..	|
38¼	**Ballintra**	,,	..	..	..	8 46	|	..	..	4 15	..	|
36½	Bridgetown	,,	..	..	..	*	|	..	..	*	..	|
34¾	Laghey	,,	..	..	..	9 1	|	..	..	4 30	..	|
33	Drumbar Halt	,,	..	..	..	—	|	..	..	—	..	|
	Donegal	,,	..	..	..	9 10	Y	..	..	4 40	..	Y
	Donegal	dep.	..	..	..	..	9 20	..	*1 15*	..	..	5
29½	Clar Bridge Halt	,,	..	..	..	..	*	..	—	..	..	*
27½	**Lough Eske**	,,	..	..	..	..	9 30	..	*1 30*	..	..	5 10
25½	Barnesmore Halt	,,	..	..	..	..	*	..	—	..	..	*
21½	Derg Bridge Halt	,,	..	..	..	..	*	..	—	..	..	*
16¼	Meen Glas Halt	,,	..	..	..	..	—	..	—	..	..	—
13¾	**Stranorlar**	arr.	..	..	..	..	10 15	..	*2 15*	..	..	5 55
	BRANCH.											
38¼	**Glenties**	dep.	LINE CLOSED on and from 15th April, 1921.	..	..	..	|	..	|	..	..	|
34¾	Shallogans Halt	,,		..	..	..	|	..	|	..	..	|
29¾	**Fintown**	,,		..	..	..	|	..	|	..	..	|
27	Ballinamore	,,		..	..	..	|	..	|	..	..	|
20½	Cloghan	,,		..	..	..	|	..	|	..	..	|
17¼	Glenmore	,,		..	..	..	|	..	|	..	..	|
14¼	Ballybofey	,,		..	..	..	|	..	|	..	..	|
	Stranorlar	arr.		..	..	..	Y	..	Y	..	..	Y
	Stranorlar	dep.	..	..	8 55	..	10 20	11 15	*2 20*	..	..	6 5
9¾	Killygordon	,,	..	..	9 5	..	10 30	*	—	..	..	6 15
8¼	Liscooly	,,	..	..	9 11	..	*	*	—	..	..	*
6¼	**Castlefinn**	,,	..	..	9 17	..	10 43	*	*2 40*	..	..	6 27
4½	Clady	,,	..	..	9 24	..	10 48	*	*	..	..	6 33
	Strabane	arr.	..	..	9 35	..	11 0	12 25	*3 0*	..	..	6 45
	MIDLAND RY. N.C.C.											
	Strabane	dep.	..	..	9 40	..	..	12 30	3 30	..	..	..
2¾	Ballymagorry	,,	..	..	9 49	..	..	12 45	3 40	..	..	..
4¼	B'heather Halt	,,	..	..	—	..	..	—	*	..	..	..
6¼	**Donemana**	,,	..	..	10 2	..	..	1 10	3 58	..	..	..
8¼	Cullion	,,	..	..	10 10	..	..	1 25	4 3	..	..	..
9¼	Desertone Halt	,,	..	..	—	..	..	—	*	..	..	..
[illegible]	New Buildings	,,	..	..	10 22	..	..	—	4 17	..	..	..
14½	**Derry (V.R.)**	arr.	..	..	10 30	..	..	1 40	4 25	..	..	..

* Will call to pick up or set down Passengers if required. Guard to keep a sharp look-out approaching.

For Crossing arrangements see page 2.

☞ **The times allowed for the running of the trains on the Strabane and Derry Section must not, under any circumstances, be reduced.**

infamous Donemana accident in 1913, when the inebriated crew put the train into the loop at around 40 mph. That 1913 service saw the introduction of a second train, the 7.45 a.m. ex-Derry and the 8.15 p.m. ex-Strabane.

Weekday services between Derry and Strabane were reduced to four trains in each direction by the end of the first war, and this lasted until the mid-1930s. It was a poor service, obviously suffering from the competition of the broad-gauge Great Northern line between the two places. On the narrow-gauge, the last up working left Strabane as early as 3.20 p.m., the last down ex-Derry at 4.50 p.m. Until then, the first train of the day started from Derry. About 1934 the Derry engine shed was shut, and the service cut back to three trains, 7.55 and 11.5 a.m. and 3.10 p.m. ex-Stranorlar, 10 a.m., 2.00 and 6.30 p.m. ex-Derry. This service continued practically unchanged for 20 years, through World War II, and up to the closing of the line. Derry was a coaling point, and the line was always worked by steam power. After the scrapping of the Class 2 engines, the turntable was not needed, and it was then removed to Rossnowlagh for railcars.

Between Strabane and Letterkenny there were three trains on weekdays from the opening date until 1916, with extra workings on Letterkenny and Raphoe Fair days. The 1917 timetable shows a reduction to two trains, leaving Letterkenny at 8.5 a.m. and 7 p.m., and Strabane at the awkward hours of 11.10 a.m. and midday. 1918 saw an even more peculiar service, with the last train of the day leaving Letterkenny at 1.15 p.m., though Fair days still had their quota of special workings. It was not until 1922 that three trains were restored, and not until the spring of 1927 that a fourth train augmented the service. The inter-state boundary resulted in the need for various parcel trains between Strabane and Lifford. About 1933, with railcar working well established, the service further improved with five workings in and out of Letterkenny. During and after World War II the line continued to be busy; in summer 1948, for instance, there were five railcars and one steam passenger train in each direction, as well as a daily steam goods. The final services prior to closure consisted of six railcars each way, plus two steam goods. For some years, after October 1949, a railcar ran out from Strabane at 3.30 a.m. to convey mails to Letterkenny, where it arrived at 5 a.m. the slow timing being due to the fact that the railcar crew looked after the level crossing gates en route.

The impact of The Troubles resulted in a 'Temporary Working Timetable' being issued as from 1 May 1921. In it the Glenties line is marked as 'closed on and after 12th April'. The branch was not reopened until 25 July 1921.

Apart from the timetable trains, excursions were popular, and were run in connection with the Hibernian and Orange demonstrations, the annual excursion of the employees of the Convoy woollen mills, religious pilgrimages, Sunday School outings and bank holidays. The hiring fairs at Letterkenny in May and November, and the Oldtown cattle fair at Letterkenny in June all got a special working in the morning out from Strabane, returning about 2 p.m. The summer excursion trains to Ballyshannon were invariably well patronised and had as many as 16 carriages, steam hauled. Double-heading, and banking, was a typical accompaniment of these gala occasions. Steam haulage on the Donegal was at its most magnificent when one of these double-headed trains tackled the steep gradient from Lough Eske into the confines of the Barnesmore Gap in the still of a summer evening.

North of the area served by the Donegal Company is the Doon Well near Kilmacrenan. This well-known holy well, is visited each summer by hundreds of pilgrims attracted by its curative properties. Standing like a sentinel over it is the Rock of Doon, an impressive crag where the chieftains of Tirconnail were inaugurated. Although the Doon Well was in the territory of the Lough Swilly Railway, the Donegal occasionally ran organised excursions to Kilmacrenan, in which their own carriages were worked through, but were hauled

Glenties	dep.	8-0 a.m.	Letterkenny	dep.	6-20 p.m.
Shallogans		8-5	Glenmaquin		pass
Fintown		8-25	Raphoe		pass
Ballinamore		8-30	Strabane	arr.	7-20
Cloghan		8-50		dep.	7-30
Glenmore		9-0	Clady		7-40
Ballybofey		pass	Castlefinn		7-50 †
Stranorlar	arr.	9.10 *	Liscooly		7-55
	dep.	9-15	Killygordon		8-0
Killygordon		9-25	Stranorlar	arr.	8-10
Liscooly		9-30		dep.	8-15
Castlefinn		9-35	Ballybofey		pass
Clady		9-40	Glenmore		8-25
Strabane	arr.	9-50	Cloghan		8-35
	dep.	10-0	Ballinamore		8-55
Raphoe		pass	Fintown		9-5
Glenmaquin		pass	Shallogans		9-20
Letterkenny	arr.	11-0	Glenties	arr.	9-25

* Cross 8.30 a.m. ex-Strabane		† Cross 7.30 p.m. ex-Stranorlar

by Swilly motive power from Letterkenny. The Donegal timing of such a special, run on Sunday 3 August 1913, appears on page 113.

The engine to work these trains was attached to the 4.40 p.m. ex-Stranorlar on Saturday 2 August, and was stabled at Glenties overnight. Inspector Farrell accompanied the train, which was to have a maximum of 10 vehicles. Foreman Quinn of Glenties acted as guard. After return to Glenties, the engine ran light to Stranorlar, where it was due at 10.40 p.m.

The annual Inspection of the Line was an important affair that extended over two days. Members of the Joint Committee started on their travels in 1914 on 10 June. An empty train had worked up from Stranorlar an hour before. They left Strabane at 10.35 a.m. and called at all stations to Letterkenny where they arrived at 11.35 a.m., and left at 11.50 a.m. A stop was made at Raphoe to cross the 12 noon ex-Strabane, and that town was reached at 12.45 p.m. for a stop of 30 minutes, and lunch. The Finn Valley stations were then taken in turn, and Stranorlar reached at 1.50 p.m. There the stop lasted for 25 minutes, for inspection, and to cross with the noon train ex-Killybegs. Only Meenglas, Derg Bridge and Barnesmore were called at, and the train then ran through Donegal town to make the next stop at Port Halt. Port was left at 3.29 p.m., Dunkineely, Bruckless and Ardara Road were inspected, and Killybegs was reached at 3.55 p.m. Inspection there would be suitably combined with refreshment, and the train set off again at 4.50 p.m. much to the relief of the entire station staff. A non-stop run was made to Inver, then Doorin Road, Mountcharles and Killymard were taken in their turn. Killymard was left at 5.47 p.m., the train again ran through Donegal, on to the Ballyshannon branch, and halted at Ballintra only, before reaching Ballyshannon at 6.35 p.m. The Ballintra call was merely to cross with the 5.30 p.m. out of Ballyshannon, inspection came the following day.

Once in Ballyshannon, conveyance was provided for the party across to the Great Northern Railway station, whence they went to Bundoran for the night at the Great Northern Hotel there. On the following day, the party left Ballyshannon at 10.20 a.m. and stopped at all stations and halts, to arrive in Donegal at 11.10 a.m. After 25 minutes there, calls were made at Clar Bridge and Lough Eske before Stranorlar received a five-minute call. Then away again and up the Glenties line to call everywhere and reach the terminus at 1.40 p.m. That must have been the lunch stop, there were 35 minutes available before the return journey began. They had seen all there was to see, a non-stop run to Strabane concluded the event.

They reached there at 3.40 p.m. and went their various ways.

The periodical fairs and markets provided much traffic, both in passengers and in cattle, horses and sheep. Monthly appendices to the working timetables were issued, giving details of the arrangements to be made. Efforts were constantly made to attract traffic away from the Swilly's line: at the Fintown Fair 'Special efforts to be made to get Letterkenny line stock via Strabane', at the Glenties Fair 'Agent to canvass the Fair. A special effort to be made to secure Letterkenny line stock' and at the Dunkineely Fair 'Agent to canvass the Fair . . . a special effort to be made to secure Letterkenny line stock via Strabane'. There was hardly a day when there was not a fair, if not actually at a station on the Committee's line, then at least in the hinterland. Specials were not often needed, but the existing trains were suitably strengthened, and for the more remote fairs the nearest station was warned 'to have wagons in readiness if traffic offers'. The arrangements during March 1913 serve as an example:

1 March, Saturday	- Ardara and Stranorlar Fairs
3 March, Monday	- Ballyshannon and Fintown Fairs
6 March, Thursday	- Strabane, Killybegs and Kinlough Fairs
8 March, Saturday	- Letterkenny Fair (special run from Strabane)
12 March, Wednesday	- Manorhamilton and Glenties Fairs
14 March, Friday	- Carrick Fair
15 March, Saturday	- Ramelton Fair, Raphoe Fair & Market (special run)
17 March, Monday	- Dunkineely and Belleek Fairs
19 March, Wednesday	- Brockagh (Cloghan) Fair
20 March, Thursday	- Grange Fair
21 March, Friday	- Killeter Fair
22 March, Saturday	- Mountcharles Fair
24 March, Monday	- Milford and Ballintra Fairs
26 March, Wednesday	- Kilcar Fair
28 March, Friday	- Castlederg Fair

During the summer, the excitement of the fairs was supplemented by other events. Thus in August 1913 there was:

3 August, Sunday	- Doon Well excursion from Glenties
4 August, Monday	- Killybegs Regatta and Sports. Bank Holiday excursion tickets to Derry, Belfast and Dublin
6 August, Wednesday	- Excursion tickets to Unionist Demonstration, Omagh
10 August, Sunday	- Clady A.O.H. Excursion to Ballyshannon (special train)
12 August, Tuesday	- Excursion tickets to Derry for Relief of Derry Celebration
17 August, Sunday	- Strabane A.O.H. Excursion to Killybegs (special train)

County Donegal Railways.

RELIEF OF DERRY

Anniversary,
Monday, 12th August, 1929.

On this date, Special Cheap Day Tickets will be issued to Derry by forenoon Trains, as under :—

STRANORLAR	- -	**2/6**
KILLYGORDON LISCOOLEY CASTLEFIN CLADY	-	**2/0**
LIFFORD BALLINDRAIT COOLAGHEY RAPHOE	-	**1/6**
CONVOY CORNAGILLAGH GLENMAQUIN	-	**1/9**

Spend the Day
in Derry.

Stranorlar 3 8 29   HENRY FORBES, Manager.

DONEGAL — 4/0   Kee & Sons. Printers Donegal   *Bshannon dn* } *5/0*
GLENMORE — 3/0   *Neyhys din* }

Handbill issued on 3 August 1929 to advertise Special Cheap Day tickets to Derry on the occasion of the annual commemoration of the Relief of the Siege of Derry. Printed in black on red. Manuscript notes of fares from other parts of the system, in the writing of Henry Forbes, are at the bottom margin

Soon after Henry Forbes' arrival, the sequence of working time-tables and their appendices began to carry the stamp of his organising ability and enthusiasm. His first working timetable came into force on 1 January 1911, a red card cover enclosing eight pages. In May it was followed by 'No. 2 Issue', 20 pages in a blue cover, with details of working regulations following the timetables. No. 3 Issue came in October 1911 and was similarly expanded, being bound in a cream cover. Thereafter, the timetable was issued annually, growing to 34 pages by No. 7 Issue in July 1915, the covers alternating from red to blue to avoid confusion.

From 1912, the official 'Appendix to the Working Time Table' was distributed monthly, usually a six-page list of fairs, special trains, and a brief note of train alterations. During 1916, these Appendices contained the working timetable in addition.

In January 1917 and January 1918, No. 8 and No. 9 issues of the working timetables were published as substantial, card-covered, 38-page booklets, coloured red and blue respectively. The dates of issue of Nos. 14 to 20 are not known, but the frequency of appearance certainly increased, for these seven issues are crowded into the short space of 24 months, No. 21 being dated January 1921. During the period of The Troubles at least one 'Temporary Working Timetable' was issued and No. 23 Issue is one such, dated May 1921 and reduced to only six pages.

From 1922 the Working Time Table settled down to the familiar paper edition of either six or eight pages, bearing a title page but no cover. Latterly there were only four pages. At first these issues contained lists of fairs and markets and information on the make-up of trains, but in later years only timetable information was given. The Appendix had now become a separate booklet, with a deep-red, card cover, and successive issues appeared in June 1923, July 1927, January 1935, January 1939 and June 1950, they varied from 20 to 26 pages and contained operating instructions only, notices of special trains and fairs being issued as duplicated pages of typescript.

The last working timetables were:

No. 102 Issue - from Sunday 28 September 1958
No. 103 Issue - from Wednesday 1 April 1959
No. 104 Issue - from Monday 22 June 1959
No. 105 Issue - from Monday 5 October 1959

For a period of about three years, the working timetables were characterised by what might be termed Henry Forbes' marginal exhortations to the staff. These were printed in bold type, and No.

49 Issue contained a typical selection : '**Ask your friends to patronise our services** / **Are you looking for new business** / **When a horse is busy kicking he's not busy pulling - do you see it?** / **Advertise the system by talking about it** / **Be courteous to the travelling public, they help to pay your wages** / **It's the little things that count, to the public and the railway** / **Speed up traffic - some one is waiting on the goods!** / **Please use the telephone and write less** / **Please write less and use the telephone** / **Please use the telephone to promptly adjust errors &c.** / **Please use the telephone for speeding up traffic** / **Overcome difficulties, there's always a way out** / **Don't offend a customer - keep smiling and help him** / **A good safe traffic rule on the road of life - when you meet temptation, turn to the right** /.' This was Forbes at his best, full of enthusiasm for the success of his railway and determined to inspire the staff to give of their best. Curran in his turn, continued the tradition. To the very last issue, the title pages of the working timetables contained : **It is well for each Member of this Railway to bear in mind that goodwill based upon years of conscientious effort may be entirely destroyed by a moment's carelessness or indifference towards a customer.**

Banking assistance through sections was permitted officially at three places : from Stranorlar to the summit near Lough Mourne, from Lough Eske to Derg Bridge Halt, and from Donegal station to Mountcharles station. The banking engine was always to be coupled to the train. The electric staff for the section was carried on board the train engine, and a special banking ticket, coloured red, was tied round the staff over its rings by the signalman. The driver of the train engine showed this staff to the driver of the banker, who was himself provided with a special banking-engine pass, coloured blue. Being coupled, the banker could not be detached from the train while in motion, but when the banked train reached the summit it stopped, the banker was uncoupled and it returned immediately to the block station from which it had set out. On arrival there the blue pass was handed to the signalman. Meanwhile the train continued to the block station in advance, where the driver handed in his red-labelled staff. The signalman who received it was not permitted to replace it in the instrument until assurance had been received over the telephone from his opposite number in the rear that the banker had cleared the section.

While banking, the rear engine carried a green tailboard, and a green (later one green and one red) lamp. Returning to base, it carried the same lamps as a train. Banking was not permitted over the Derry road.

THE
STRABANE AND LETTERKENNY RAILWAY.

(WORKED BY JOINT COMMITTEE.)

DOWN TRAINS.—Week Days.

STATIONS.		S. Mails only	M.	M.	S.	M.	T. Goods only	M.	S.	M. Mails only	S.	M.
		a.m.	a.m.	a.m.	a.m.	p.m.	p.m.	p.m.	p.m.	p.m.	p.m.	p.m.
Strabane	dep.	7 20	7 50	10 50	11 45	1 25	2 35	4 30	4 55	6 36		7 25
Lifford Halt	arr.	7 22	7 52	10 52	11 47	1 27	2 37	4 32	4 57	6 38		7 27
Lifford Halt	dep.		8 0	10 55	12 5	1 30		4 35	5 0			7 30
Ballindrait	arr.		*	*	*	*		*	*		6 0	*
Coolaghy Halt	dep.		*	*	*	*		*	*		*	*
Raphoe	„		8 20	11 12	12 27	1 50		4 55	5 30		6 50	7 50
Convoy	„		8 28	11 20	12 35	1 51		5 3			7 0	7 58
Cornagillagh Halt	„		*	*	*	*		*			*	*
Glenmaquin	„		*	*	*	*		*			*	*
Letterkenny	arr.		8 55	11 45	1 4	2 22		5 30			7 30	8 25

UP TRAINS.—Week Days.

STATIONS.		S. Mails only	M.	M.	T. Goods only	S.	S.	M.	S.	M. Mails only	M.	M.
		a.m.	a.m.	a.m.	p.m.	p.m.	p.m.	p.m.	p.m.	p.m.	p.m.	p.m.
Letterkenny	dep.		9 30	11 50		1 5	2 25	3 5			6 15	8 30
Glenmaquin	„		*	*		*	*	*			*	*
Cornagillagh Halt	„		*	*		*	*	*			*	*
Convoy	„		10 0	12 18		1 40	2 55	3 35			6 40	*
Raphoe	„		10 10	12 28		1 50	3 5	3 43	5 35		6 48	*
Coolaghy Halt	„		*	*		*	*	*	*		*	*
Ballindrait	„		*	*	1 50	*	*	*	5 50		*	*
Lifford Halt	„	7 28	10 28	12 43	2 33	2 13	3 28	4 3		6 40	7 8	9 28
Strabane	arr.	7 30	10 30	12 45	2 55	2 15	3 30	4 5		6 42	7 10	9 30

* Steam Trains will call to pick up or set down Passengers if required. Driver and Guard to keep a sharp look-out approaching.

The 11.45 a.m. ex Strabane to cross 11.50 a.m. ex Letterkenny at Raphoe and 1.5 p.m. at Letterkenny.
The 1.25 p.m. ex Strabane to cross 1.5 p.m. ex Letterkenny at Raphoe and 2.25 p.m. at Letterkenny.
The 6.15 p.m. ex Letterkenny to cross 6.0 p.m. ex Ballindrait at Raphoe.

COMPOSITION OF TRAINS.

All trains carrying passengers must have coaches next engine with wagons on rear, except that Convoy wagons from Strabane, Lifford, and Raphoe may be placed next engine. Also Customs wagons from Strabane off at Lifford for examination to be placed next engine.

REQUIREMENTS OF GOVERNMENT DEPARTMENTS.

Stations have clear and definite instructions as to carrying out of these, relating to the conveyance ertain traffics and Customs Regulations which must be strictly complied with.

STRANORLAR,
JUNE, 1934.

HENRY FORBES,
Manager.

DOWN TRAINS—WEEK DAYS.

M—RAIL MOTORS. T—TRACTOR. S—STEAM TRAINS (Goods and Passengers).

Distance from Strabane.	STATIONS.	M.	M.	M.	S.	M.	M.	S.	S.	M.	S.	S.	M.	T.	M.	S.	S.	M.	M.	M.	S.	M.	
		a.m.	a.m.	a.m.	a.m.	a.m.	p.m.	p.m.	p.m.	p.m.	p.m.	p.m.	p.m.	p.m.	p.m.	p.m.	p.m.	p.m.	p.m.	p.m.	p.m.	p.m.	p
	L.M.S. (N.C.C.)																						
14½	Derry (V.R.) dep.				10 0											2 0					6 30		
11¾	New Buildings ,,				10 9											2 9					6 39		
9¾	Desertone Halt ,,				*											*					*		
8¼	Cullion ,,				10 20											2 20					6 50		
6¼	Donemana ,,				10 28											2 28					6 58		
4¼	B'heather Halt ,,				*											*					—		
2¾	Ballymagorry ,,				10 41											2 41					7 11		
	Strabane arr.				10 50											2 50					7 20		
	Strabane dep.	7 50				11 0			11 45	1 15				3 15			4 30	6 0				7 25	[illegible]
4½	Clady ,,	*				11 10			*	*				*			*	6 10				*	
6	Castlefinn arr.	8 6				11 15			12 5	1 30				3 45			4 50	6 15				*	
	Castlefinn dep.	8 8				11 30			12 25	1 35				4 20			5 0	6 20				*	
8	Liscooly ,,	*				*			*	*				*			*	*				*	
9¾	Killygordon ,,	8 20				11 41			*	*				*			*	6 30				*	
11¾	Cavan Halt ,,	*				*			*	*				*			*	*				*	
13¼	Town Bridge ,,	*				*			*	*				*			*	*				*	
13½	Stranorlar arr.	8 30				11 50			12 50	2 0				5 0			5 20	6 40				8 0	[illegible]
	BRANCH.																						
	Stranorlar dep.		8 40				12 0					2 20							6 45				
14	Ballybofey ,,		*				*					*							*				
17¾	Glenmore ,,		8 52				*					*							*				
20½	Cloghan ,,		9 0				*					2 50							*				
23	Elatagh Halt ,,		*				*					*							*				
27	Ballinamore ,,		*				*					*							*				
29¾	Fintown ,,		9 25				12 50					3 15							7 35				
34½	Shallogans Halt ,,		*				*					*							*				
38	Glenties arr.	Y	9 50			Y	1 10				Y	3 35					Y	Y	7 55				
	Stranorlar dep.	8 35				11 55					2 5		3 40				5 50	6 45					
21½	Derg Bridge Halt ,,	*				*					*		*				*	*					
25½	Barnesmore Halt ,,	*				*					*		*				*	*					
27½	Lough Eske arr.	9 14				*					*		*				*	*					
	Lough Eske dep.	9 16				*					*		*				*	*					
29½	Clar Bridge Halt ,,	*				*					*		*				*	*					
31½	Donegal arr.	9 26				12 43					2 50		4 25				6 40	7 30					
	BRANCH.																						
	Donegal dep.			9 30				1 15					5 30							7 40			
33	Drumbar Halt ,,			*				*					*							*			
34¾	Laghey ,,			9 39				*					*							*			
36¼	Bridgetown ,,			9 45				*					*							*			
38½	Ballintra ,,			9 50				1 35					5 50							8 5			
39½	Dromore Halt ,,			*				*					*							*			
41¾	Rossnowlagh ,,			10 0				1 45					6 0							8 15			
42½	Coolmore Halt ,,			*				*					*							*			
44¼	Creevy Halt ,,			*				*					*							*			
47	Ballyshannon arr	Y		10 10		Y		2 0					6 15				Y	Y		8 25			
	Donegal dep.	9 30				12 48									5 0		7 0	7 40					
35½	Mountcharles ,,	9 43				1 2									*		*	*					
37¼	Doorin Road Halt ,,	*				*									*		*	*					
38¾	Mullanboy Halt ,,	*				*									*		*	*					
39¾	Inver ,,	9 55				1 14									5 25		7 30	8 5					
41¼	Port Halt ,,	*				*									*		*	*					
43¾	Dunkineely ,,	10 10				1 28									*		*	*					
46	Bruckless ,,	*				*									*		*	*					
48¾	Ardara Road Halt ,,	*				*									*		*	*					
50¾	Killybegs arr.	10 30				1 48									6 0		8 5	8 40					

* Steam Trains will call to pick up or set down Passengers if required,

CROSSING

1.15 p.m. ex Strabane to cross 12.50 p.m. ex Stranorlar at Castlefin and 11.40 a.m. ex Killybegs at Stranorlar.
7.50 a.m. ex Strabane cross 8.33 a.m. at Stranorlar and 7.50 a.m. ex Killybegs at Lough Eske.
11.0 a.m. ex Strabane cross 12 ncon at Stranorlar, 11.40 a.m. ex Killybegs at Donegal, and 1.50 p.m. at Killybegs.
11.45 a.m. ex Strabane cross 12.0 noon ex Stranorlar at Castlefin and 12.50 p.m. at Stranorlar.
12.0 noon ex Stranorlar cross 12.30 p.m. ex Glenties at Fintown.
2.5 p.m. ex Stranorlar cross 1.50 p.m. ex Killybegs at Donegal.
3.15 p.m. Tractor ex Strabane cross 11.40 a.m. ex Killybegs at Strabane and 1.50 p.m. ex Killybegs at Castlefin.

UP TRAINS—WEEK DAYS.

M—RAIL MOTORS.   T—TRACTOR.   S—STEAM TRAINS (Goods and Passengers).

STATIONS	M a.m.	S a.m.	M a.m.	S a.m.	M a.m.	M a.m.	S a.m.	M a.m.	M noon	T p.m.	S p.m.	S p.m.	S p.m.	M p.m.	S p.m.	M p.m.	M p.m.	M p.m.	M p.m.	M p.m.	M p.m.
Killybegs dep.						7 50							11 40	1 50				3 45	6 5		
Ardara Road "																					
Bruckless "																		3 57			
Dunkineely "													12 0					4 5			
Port Halt "																					
Inver "						8 25							12 15	2 25				4 20	6 40		
Mullanboy Halt "																					
Doorin Road "																					
Mountcharles "													12 30					4 33			
Donegal arr.						8 50							12 42	2 50				4 45	7 0		
Ballyshannon dep							8 10					12 0					4 0				6 50
Creevy Halt "																					
Coolmore Halt "																					
Rossnowlagh "							8 25					12 15					4 15				7 5
Dromore Halt "																					
Ballintra "							8 35					12 25					4 25				7 15
Bridgetown "																					
Laghey "																					
Drumbar Halt "																					
Donegal "							8 55					12 45					4 50				7 35
Donegal dep.						9 5							1 5	2 52	4 25			5 5			7 40
Clar Bridge Halt "																					
Lough Eske arr.						9 14												5 14			
Lough Eske dep.						9 15												5 15			
Barnesmore Halt "																					
Derg Bridge Halt "																					
Stranorlar arr.						9 53							1 55	3 37	5 10			5 50	8 30		
Glenties dep.		7 20						10 35				12 30					4 45				
Shallogans Halt "																					
Fintown "		7 45						11 0				12 55					5 5				
Ballinamore "																					
Elatagh Halt "																					
Cloghan "								11 25				1 25					5 30				
Glenmore "																	5 38				
Ballybofey "																					
Stranorlar arr.		8 30						11 50				1 45					5 55				
Stranorlar dep.	7 0			8 33		9 55		12 0	12 50				2 0	3 40			6 0				8 10
Town Bridge "																					
Cavan Halt "																					
Killygordon "				8 43		10 5							2 10				6 10				
Liscooly "																					
Castlefinn arr.				8 53		10 15		12 20	1 25				2 20				6 19				
Castlefinn dep.				8 54		10 16		12 22	2 15				2 35				6 20				
Clady "				8 58		10 21											6 25				
Strabane arr.	7 30			9 8		10 30		12 40	2 35				2 50	4 15			6 34				8 45
Strabane dep.		7 35					11 5						3 15								
Ballymagorry "		7 44					11 15						3 24								
B'heather Halt "																					
Donemana "		7 58					11 32						3 38								
Cullion "		8 6											3 46								
Desertone Halt "																					
New Buildings "		8 18											3 58								
Derry (V.R.) arr.		8 25					12 0						4 5								

BRANCH (Ballyshannon–Donegal); *BRANCH* (Glenties–Stranorlar); *L.M.S. (N.C.C.)* (Strabane–Derry); *SATURDAYS ONLY* (last column).

Drivers and Guard to keep a sharp look out approaching.

ARRANGEMENTS.

3.40 p.m. ex Stranorlar cross 1.50 p.m. ex Killybegs at Stranorlar and 4.25 p.m. ex Donegal at Donegal.

5.0 p.m. ex Donegal cross 3.45 p.m. ex Killybegs at Donegal.

4.30 p.m. ex Strabane cross 3.45 p.m. ex Killybegs at Stranorlar, and 6.5 p.m. ex Killybegs at Donegal.

6.0 p.m. ex Strabane cross 3.45 p.m. ex Killybegs at Castlefinn and 6.50 p.m. ex Ballyshannon at Donegal.

7.40 p.m. ex Donegal cross 6.50 p.m. ex Ballyshannon at Donegal.

Banking assistance was not in fact used greatly except for the heavy summer excursion trains, but the procedure was followed in the summer of 1943-4, when a railcar was attached to the rear of the 4.50 p.m. Stranorlar—Donegal mixed train, merely for convenience and to avoid a separate empty railcar working. The car was detached at Derg Bridge, picked up men who had been cutting peat in the Company's bog there, and returned to Stranorlar.

During the last 30 years' working the tonnage of merchandise moved over the system ranged from around 90,000 tons per year to around half that figure. Of these totals, only from a fifth to a third originated on the system, so that much of it consisted of materials imported into the county. In the opposite direction the bulk of the traffic was of livestock.

Until lorry traffic developed, the railway was the main distributor of coal, which came in through the ports of Derry and Killybegs, and even in the earliest days of the FVR the Stranorlar coal-merchant stored his wares by the railway yard. Turf traffic was always small, since the turf banks, where it was cut and dried, were usually sited near their owner's house. However, wartime coal shortages led to more widespread peat cutting and converted six-wheel and bogie wagons were used to handle the bulky if light loads from the banks near the Glenties line and near Derg Bridge.

The hoped-for stone traffic of Barnesmore granite never materialised since the stone was not suited for dressing into building blocks. Nearby the Gap, however, the Derg Bridge siding took out a large tonnage of gravel for concrete aggregate during the construction of the Erne barrage at Ballyshannon. The Mountcharles quarries gave rise to a traffic in freestone for some years after the Killybegs section was opened, and for a time Mountcharles station had a five-ton crane to handle it.

The bulk of the merchandise traffic originating on the system consisted of grain and potatoes. What the official returns listed as 'Ale & Porter (including empties)' was always a significant fraction of the traffic, and the loading of Guinness barrels, empty and full, was a familiar sight at all stations. Eggs formed a Donegal export, and in 1931 their tonnage rose to 1,465.

Livestock traffic practically all moved in an outward direction. In 1930, 41,000 head were carried, mostly cattle and sheep. With the development of the Committee's livestock lorry service, especially in the 1950s, the numbers sent by rail dwindled greatly and had fallen to well below 1,000 head in 1958 and 1959.

As farm mechanisation progressed, various pieces of agricultural machinery came into the county, usually through Strabane. Some of the loads were awkward. One recollects a new and brightly-painted reaper and binder which unavoidably overhung its wagon side at Strabane. It was addressed to Donegal and clearance at the overbridges worried the train crew as they moved off on the FV line. Anxious glances were cast along the side of the train as it moved slowly under the road bridge at the south end of Strabane station. The clearance must have been minute, there may have been a flake of paint lost, but once through the stone arch the relief was audible, for between there and Stranorlar the broad-gauge origin of the line removed further cause for concern.

All the lines were, of course, single tracked, and worked by electric train staff. Larger-type instruments were in use on the Derry, Glenties, Ballyshannon and Killybegs lines, and miniature staffs on the Finn Valley, West Donegal and Letterkenny lines. The sections were as follows:

Strabane—Londonderry	Strabane—Donemana ⎫ Donemana—Londonderry ⎰	later Strabane— Londonderry
Finn Valley	Strabane—Castlefinn Castlefinn—Stranorlar	
West Donegal	Stranorlar—Lough Eske Lough Eske—Donegal	
Killybegs line	Donegal—Inver Inver—Killybegs	
Glenties line	Stranorlar—Fintown ⎫ Fintown—Glenties ⎰	later Stranorlar— Glenties
Ballyshannon branch	Donegal—Ballintra ⎫ Ballintra—Ballyshannon ⎰	later Donegal— Ballyshannon
Strabane & Letterkenny *line*	Strabane—Raphoe ⎫ Raphoe—Glenmaquin ⎬ Glenmaquin—Letterkenny ⎭	later Strabane— Raphoe Raphoe—Letterkenny

Sidings at stations and halts other than the block stations were operated by a key attached to the staff. The staff and its key were locked in the points lock when the points were made for the siding, and only when the points were returned to normal was the staff released.

There were 63 public road crossing gates on the system and these are listed in Table 2. Ten of the gates were connected with a down signal and 14 with an up signal, in all cases to give warning where the gates were concealed from approaching trains by a curve. All the gates carried discs, and lamps after dark, which showed red in one direction and green in the other. The crossing keepers' cottages, invariably distinguished by the name of the family which lived there, had no telephone or bell communication.

From the opening of the narrow gauge in 1894 Strabane station consisted of a single platform, facing south-east towards the Great Northern station. When the s & l was opened, a further platform face was made on the north-west side, thus converting the existing platform into an island. The station offices faced the original platform. A covered footbridge linked the GNR and CD stations, though many passengers preferred the unofficial rail-level route laid in sleepers between the ramps. As Strabane was the only station in Northern Ireland, the Imperial Customs Post was located there. A signal cabin, substantially built of brick, and very obviously of NCC design, stood between the Finn Valley and s & l lines at the south-west side of the station.

Leaving Strabane on the Finn Valley section, the line passed below the Lifford Road and immediately afterwards crossed the River Mourne by a girder bridge, set on screw piles. The GNR bridge lay a short way upstream, carrying their line to Omagh. A quarter-mile beyond the river crossing, traces of the course of the old broad-gauge FVR line could be seen on the left, trailing in from the site of Finn Valley Junction.

The course of the line was level for four miles and lay along the flat valley floor of the River Finn. The inter-state boundary between Counties Tyrone and Donegal was formed here by the river itself, which lay to the right of the line with broad areas of marshland along its banks. Some 3½ miles out from Strabane the courses of river and railway converged, and with the woods of Urney House on the left, the line crossed a girder bridge into Eire.

A mile beyond the Urney Bridge the line entered Clady station, a single platform on the right, with a one-storey cottage-type building. The Republic of Ireland Customs Preventive work was done here.

From Clady both river and railway ran almost due west, as far as Stranorlar. One and a half miles from Clady, Castlefinn was the most important intermediate station on the Finn Valley section, with two platforms, each signalled for both up and down working. Executive R. of I. Customs work was done here. In recent years at

Page 125 : RAILCARS AT WORK

(above) Lough Eske, 20 August 1959. Railcar No. 16 and van, passing Railcar No. 20; (below) Dunkineely, 31 December 1959. Railcar No. 16 and van, ex-Killybegs

Page 126: STRANORLAR—1

(above) River Finn Bridge on the Glenties branch, with Locomotive No. 3 of Class 1; (below) Aerial view, looking towards Ballybofey. The station is on the near side of the river

least, the nameboards on the two platforms differed, one side preferring 'Castlefin', the other the double 'n' ending.

Half a mile past Castlefinn the line encountered a short stretch of 1-in-125, and thereafter rose gently towards Stranorlar. Liscooly and Killygordon were simple one-platform stations. Cavan Halt consisted of a short stone-faced platform, built to serve the railcars, as was Town Bridge Halt, almost within sight of Stranorlar.

The Stranorlar yard and station extended for almost 400 yards. Coming in from Strabane, the workshops and the engine and railcar sheds were passed on the left, a substantial group of white-washed stone-built buildings. The original West Donegal engine shed had a single road, in front of which stood the water tank, with a small turntable beside it. This original shed later became the loco repair shop, with the West Donegal carriage shed and the Finn Valley carriage shed together forming the three-gable-ended building that in Joint Committee days was the workshop. The later and larger engine shed had three roads, and stood separately to the south.

The down platform, on the left of the through road, started from a whitewashed stone building used as a carriage shed by the West Donegal, but later made into the General Stores. This down platform curved towards the river crossing, and ended near the West signal cabin. An iron footbridge, with massive stone steps at each end, linked the down and up platforms.

The up platform was partly roofed. Alongside it were the station buildings and the administrative offices of the companies. Diamond-paned windows and heavy stone arches gave this old Finn Valley headquarters a distinctly exotic but picturesque appearance. For many years the offices occupied by the manager and engineer were in the upper floor of the main building, but in later years the staff worked in the low building between the old headquarters and the river bank.

Entering the station from the yard, passengers found themselves in a hallway: the booking office on the left and a refreshment counter on the right, behind which tea was made to order on a tiny iron range.

The Glenties line diverged as a single road from the main line immediately in front of the offices, and curved fairly sharply towards the river crossing.

Leaving Stranorlar on the West Donegal section, the line curved to the left and on a southerly course crossed the River Finn by a viaduct of four girder spans with arched masonry approaches. Once

County Donegal Railways Joint Committee

CHRISTMAS ARRANGEMENTS
1959

With the following exceptions, the usual Services will operate during the Christmas period.

(See Separate Handbill for particulars of Omnibus Service).

Monday 14th to Saturday 19th December, (incl.)

Additional Trains will run as under:—

		p.m.	p m.			p m.
Letterkenny	dep.	7.25	9.0	Strabane	dep.	7.35
Strabane	arr.	8.28	10.15	Letterkenny	arr	8.35

Sunday 20th December.

Usual Church Services will run on Ballyshannon Section only

Monday 21st December to Wednesday 23rd December.

The following Trains will NOT run:—

4.51 p.m Stranorlar to Donegal

An additional Train will run as under:—

		p m.	p.m.			p.m.	p.m.			p.m
Strabane	dep.	6.15	7.30	Letterkenny	dep.	7.25	9.0	Strabane	dep	7.3
Stranorlar	arr.	6.55	8.10	Strabane	arr	8.28	10.15	Letterkenny	arr	8 3
Donegal	arr.	8.5								

Thursday 24th December.

Services will be as on Saturdays, with the following additions:—

		p.m.			p.m.			p.m.
Donegal	dep.	8.5	Letterkenny	dep.	9.0	Strabane	dep.	10.40
Stranorlar	arr.	9.5	Strabane	arr.	10.15	Letterkenny	arr	11.45

Friday 25th December and Sunday 27th December.

Usual Church Services will run on Ballyshannon Section only

Saturday 26th December.

No Services will operate

Monday 28th December to Thursday 31st December, 1959, (incl.)

Usual Services will operate, with the following additions:—

		p.m.			p.m.
Letterkenny	dep	7.25	Strabane	dep.	7.35
Strabane	arr.	8.28	Letterkenny	arr.	8.35

Stranorlar,
23/11/1959.

B. L. CURRAN
Manager and Secretary

The County Donegal goes down fighting. This handbill, printed in black on yellow paper, and measuring 10" x 7", advertised the traffic arrangements during the last two weeks of the life of the railway

across the river, the line turned right, set a westerly course and began the long climb towards Barnesmore Gap, rising about 550 ft over a distance of eight miles. The first mile of the ascent was at 1-in-59. One and a half miles at 1-in-50 followed to Meenglas Halt, a platform and shelter on the left side. Here the traveller was able on a clear day to catch a glimpse of the shapely cone of Errigal 22 miles away to the N.N.W., at 2,466 ft the highest of the mountains of Donegal. The line now ran across open moorland, some of it reafforested in recent years.

Beyond Meenglas, where in the early days Viscount Lifford would have left the train to drive to his house some miles to the south, the climb continued, with a further three miles at 1-in-60. Then six miles from Stranorlar, the hard work was suddenly over, and a delightful view of Lough Mourne opened out ahead. The gradient became almost level on the moorland plateau, and the line lay only a few yards from the water. Past the Lough, a short climb at 1-in-67 carried the line 30 ft up to its summit at 591 ft above sea level at Derg Bridge Halt. The mountain barrier lay ahead, gashed in spectacular fashion by the Gap.

As the line passed over the summit, and swung gently towards the left, the prospect opened up. On the left of the line, the hill of Barnesmore (1,491 ft) falls steeply in brown granite crags to the railway track, while equally steeply to the north, Croaghconnelagh (1,724 ft) forms the opposite face of the defile. At the end of the 17th century the Gap was infested with freebooters and highwaymen, and the site of the gallows where many of them met justice is still pointed out.

Plunging down through the Gap, the road, which kept the line company near the summit, dropped away steeply and was soon far below it. The ruling gradient on the descent was 1-in-64 for the first mile, steepening to 1-in-60 for the next 2½ miles, and a short way from Barnesmore Halt slackening to 1-in-144. All the way through the Gap the line ran on a shelf cut along the steep southern face and the passenger had fine views of the rock-strewn slopes to the left and the valley floor, road and winding Lowerymore River on the right. By Barnesmore Halt 300 ft of height had been lost, the scenery had softened and the line plunged below the road, to continue between it and the river as far as the original West Donegal terminus of Druminin, set in the townland of that name, and later renamed Lough Eske.

A passing loop was provided at Lough Eske, immediately to the east of the station. A picturesque spot, it was backed by a plantation

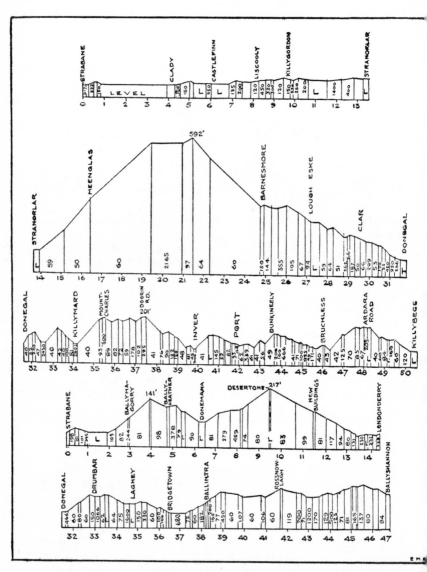

These gradient diagrams, with their vertical scale greatly exaggerated, illustrate the remarkable topographic contrasts of the country traversed by the railway. The Strabane—Stranorlar section, never far from the River Finn, was practically level. From Stranorlar to Donegal the crossing of the Blue Stack Mountains through the Barnesmore Gap accounted for the long

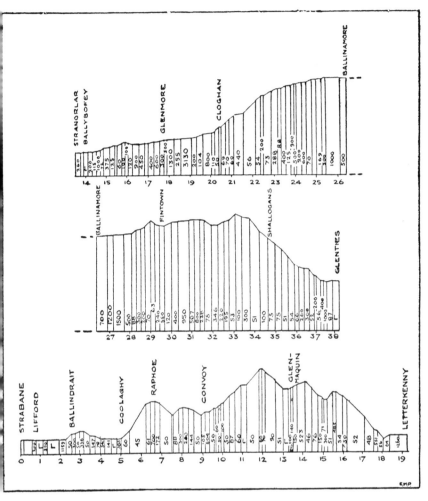

gradients, with the run beside Lough Mourne making the level stretch near the summit.

The effects of drumlin topography is seen in both the Donegal—Killybegs and the Donegal—Ballyshannon diagrams. Unlike these sections, the twin gables on the Strabane—Londonderry road were not caused by drumlins but by the crossing of the north-east margin of the Sperrin Mountains.

The Glenties line, driven into the mountains some 10 miles north of Barnesmore, encountered similar topography, but had a much longer summit level. The S & L Railway had scarcely any level portions and its gabled profile is due to the numerous stream and river valleys which cut across the course of the line.

of tall pine trees, with magnificent mountain views across the valley. Just beyond the station, the road crossed the line on the level at the second set of gates since Strabane. Lough Eske itself lies to the north, splendidly situated in a mountain amphitheatre.

From Lough Eske station, the line fell through Clar Bridge Halt to Donegal town, the gradients changing frequently in a scenery of little whale-backed hills or drumlins. A few short stretches of 1-in-50 brought the line down almost to sea level at Donegal, a terminus from 1889 until 1893.

Donegal station had four platform faces, the longest two serving the down and up through roads. The south side of the down through platform had a short bay, and what was formerly the carriage-shed road formed a bay to the north of the up platform. The carriage shed originally extended 170 ft from the end of the platform to the overbridge. The latter was erected in 1908.

The stone-built, single-road engine shed, the water tank and the turntable were all on the north side of the through lines. Originally the coaling stage and permanent-way yard were also there, but latterly their site had become completely overgrown.

The Donegal station building stood on the down platform, with a capacious verandah roof supported by pillars. The agent's house, alongside, was stone-built and of two storeys. From 1889 until 1924 it had two gable ends facing the road, extensions then giving it a third gable on the west side.

A short way beyond the ends of the platforms, the line to Killybegs crossed a minor road on the level. Beyond the gates, two minor ascents over the drumlins gave short stretches of 1-in-40, a foretaste of what was to come. Killymard, a short platform to the left, lay in a hollow at the foot of the stiffest pull on the whole system, the Glen Bank of 1½ miles at 1-in-40. On the ascent the line passed below a high, three-arched overbridge. Mountcharles stood at the summit, the station buildings, typical of this stretch, of whitewashed stone with later additions of corrugated iron.

Further progress towards Killybegs was necessarily switchback in character, through the swarm of whale-backed drumlins first encountered near Lough Eske.*

The drumlins lie between the shore of Donegal Bay and the mountains to the north, and are separated by lakelets, areas of marsh and winding streams. The long axis of each drumlin in this

---

* For the reader who is interested in an appreciation of this rather unusual topography, an explanation of the origin and form of drumlins is given in *The Geology of Ireland*, by J. K. Charlesworth (Edinburgh, 1953).

particular area lies roughly north-east to south-west; they produce a rolling country, nowhere of great height, but offering difficulties to the builders of both roads and railways. The 'grain' of the country lies, in fact, at right angles to the railway.

Along this northern coast of Donegal Bay, three peninsulas extend to the south, drumlins aligned along them. Crossing one of these, the line attained its highest point (201 ft) between Donegal and Killybegs, at Doorin Road Halt. To the south, on a fine day, the mountains of Counties Sligo and Mayo formed a backcloth to the expanse of sea. From Doorin Road, a descent of 2½ miles, partly at 1-in-41—48, brought the line past Mullanboy Halt into Inver, the intermediate staff station. A loop here was removed and passing was done by backing the early arrival into the siding.

From Inver, with the shore close on the left, Port Halt came up, with its small harbour a short way below the line. Dunkineely and Bruckless followed, both originally stations and with substantial cottage-type houses, but latterly demoted to the status of halts. There were a number of stiff gradients in both directions over this stretch of line, the most severe being 1-in-40 on a 7½-chain curve at Seahill, near Dunkineely. Another stiff climb came in the down direction just after Bruckless, with threequarters of a mile at 1-in-42 up a rock cutting, where a wet rail often caused steam trains to stall on many occasions.

The halt of Ardara Road was hopefully situated at the road junction to Ardara, a village 12 miles distant, and was at the head of a land-locked bay which broadened into Killybegs Harbour, one of the best and most sheltered anchorages on the whole west coast of Ireland. Passing a fish-meal factory close to the shore, the line ran down the west side of the anchorage, past Hegarty's Gates, and into the covered, single-platform terminus, hemmed between the small town of Killybegs and the sea wall. The goods yard was between the station and the pier, with oil tanks for supplying the fishing fleet. A single road extended down the length of the pier, the rails sunk into the concrete surface.

For lack of room near the station, the one-road, one-engine shed was placed in a situation reminiscent of a boat-house, between the line and the shore, 180 yd towards Donegal town. It was stone built and about five years before the end of rail workings it was wrecked by a runaway engine, believed to be No. 6, which had brought in a special from Letterkenny. The end wall was demolished. The shed was by then little used and the walls were trimmed down to knee-level.

Between the engine shed and Killybegs station a small signal cabin was formerly perched on the sea wall, but it was later replaced by a ground frame, between the outer wall of the station and the shore.

Killybegs has a magnificent deep-water harbour, at one time considered as a port for Atlantic liners. On the exposed rock coast nearby, a ship of the Spanish Armada perished.

In steam days, Killybegs had no turntable, but for railcars one was built on the site of a loading bank, a short way beyond the platform end and the water tank. It was interesting in its Forbesian construction, for the frame was derived from one of the Class 2 engines. Later, in 1950, the frame of No. 19 took its place.

Returning to Stranorlar, the Glenties branch crossed the River Finn immediately west of the station, on a massive girder bridge with one of the largest single spans in Ireland. This bridge was reputed to have been built for a Norwegian broad-gauge line, but because of some hitch was diverted to Co. Donegal. Running close to the Finn, and with the dark woods of Drumboe on the farther bank, the line soon entered Ballybofey. For the next twenty miles the branch ascended the upper Finn valley, through wooded country for the first half, with the halts of Glenmore, Cloghan, Elatagh and Glassagh serving the scattered agricultural community. The climb eased at Fintown station, situated on the north shore of Lough Finn, the source of the river and a fine three-mile stretch of water. Across the lough, the mountains of Scraigs (1,410 ft) and Aghla (1,961 ft) rose steeply from the shore. Tradition has it that the grave of the Irish giant, Finn McCoul, lies close to the shore of Lough Finn, at the foot of Aghla.

Three miles beyond Fintown, a final climb at 1-in-320-195-53 brought the line up to the watershed, the summit being 510 ft above sea level. The branch continued for a further five miles down the Shallogan† River valley to the small market town of Glenties, through rather bare, open moorland, with some parts at 1-in-51. The road lay to the right-hand side of the line until just before the terminus.

The railway gave the folk of the upper Finn valley an excellent service, especially in railcar days, and they came to regard it with considerable affection. Its closing to passenger traffic at the end of 1947 inspired some verses*, based on the popular air 'Galway Bay':

† Also spelt 'Shallogans'.
* Published in *Derry People*, 10 January 1948, and written by Mr D. O'Kelly of Lifford.

Oh, some day I'll go back again to Glenties—
It may be at 'the closing of the line' . . .
To see once more the sun rise over Achla—
And the moonbeams on Gweebarra softly shine.

To watch the road bus rolling by the station—
And stopping at the breezy Workhouse Brae:
To mingle with the crowds there waiting patient,
And to hear the old folks sigh—and sadly say:

The lorries now bring up our little rations,
The buses seldom halt where we would go,
For we who live in glens and misty valleys,
Speak a language these Six-County lads don't know.

These strangers come and try to teach us their way—
They blame us that we are so very slow!
But they might as well grow grapes on Meenathowey
Or try rob Slieve Sneachta of its coat of snow!

The road bus roars along our quiet highways;
It kills the cows and lames the collie dog. . . .
But wait avic! this will not last forever—
'Tis soon you'll see it spluttering in the bog!

They say there is a lovely life hereafter;
If so, we all may see it very soon—
While tumbling down the braes into deep water,
As the frosty roads lie freezing 'neath the moon.

Here far away from Finntown and from Glenties
I dream of when I'll see those glens again . . .
But oh, it breaks my heart when I remember
The old days when I travelled by the train.

I see her still there waiting at Stranorlar . . .
I hear her whistling into Ballybofey . . .
The old folk speaking Irish up at Cloghan . .
And the little cottage lights along the way.

The country boys were crowding every platform,
The colleens shyly blushed beneath their shawls;
The Rosses swanks got out at Finntown station,
Where the roses ramble o'er the whitewashed walls.

The moon was shining bright on Derryloaghan—
Her shadow travelled with the little train;
There was a happy crowd at Glenties waiting . . .
But we'll never see the likes of that again!

Oh, some day I'll go back again to Glenties—
It may be in the summer or the snow . . .
But riding in the road bus I'll be lonely,
When I see that rusty railway down below.

The Ballyshannon branch left Donegal station in an easterly direction, parallel to the West Donegal line for a short way. It then turned south in a curve of 800 ft radius and entered a cutting. The Ballybofey road crossed the line on an overbridge about 40 yd south of the end of the curve and Hospital Halt was placed just beyond the bridge, a single stone platform on the left. The serious collision of 29 August 1949 took place about ten yards north of the Hospital overbridge: the goods special pushed back the railcar for 55 yd towards Donegal.

Emerging from this cutting, the line entered open country, studded with the ubiquitous drumlins and with occasional glimpses of the sea to the west. Drumbar, Laghey and Bridgetown stations, later down-graded to halts, were passed en route to Ballintra. This was formerly the ETS station midway along the branch, but for its last eight years the branch was worked as one section, and the instruments removed. The station buildings were lightly built, compared to the older sections, with shelters of matchboarding and corrugated iron. The Ballintra station agent's house was of stone.

Rossnowlagh, 3¼ miles past Ballintra, had a considerable excursion traffic, and to cope with special trains a turntable was transferred from Derry to handle both steam locomotive and railcars. Beyond Rossnowlagh, Friary Halt, Coolmore and Creevy passed in rapid succession, to bring the line into the terminus on the north side of Ballyshannon town.

The Strabane & Letterkenny line swung rapidly away from the main line after it left the north face of the island platform at Strabane. Less than half a mile out, it crossed the River Foyle, and at the same time the boundary of Co. Donegal and Co. Tyrone, by a 293 ft girder bridge. Lifford station and the R of I Customs Post lay at the north end of the bridge and sidings were provided for wagons undergoing examination. Trains also picked up and set down a considerable volume of mail here, for the Post Office sorting depot was on the station premises.

For two miles beyond Lifford the line held a level course, skirting a cluster of low hills, and curving left into the valley of the Deele River, a minor tributary of the Foyle. Ballindrait Halt was passed a short way beyond the river crossing. The line then proceeded in close company with the road to Coolaghy Halt. Ahead lay a steep bank up to Raphoe, 1¾ miles mostly at 1-in-45. Raphoe was an ETS exchange point, and for many years had a crossing loop, but after this was removed trains still crossed, using the goods siding.

Raphoe is an ancient town, once a diocesan seat. The ruins of the former bishops' palace adjoin the small cathedral. The station, and its onetime station agent, Willie Johnston, were immortalised in some verses of which unfortunately it has not been possible to obtain a complete version. But what remains seems worth quoting:

> Standing ready at the station at Raphoe,
> Doesn't matter how the morning breezes blow,
> There's the smiling face of genial Mr. Johnston
> Selling tickets as they tell him where they go.
> And there's folk there from Strabane,
> Out to smuggle all they can,
> Standing ready at the station at Raphoe.

Beyond Raphoe the line crossed the valleys of the Swilly Burn and the Deele River to reach Convoy station, serving a town which has a flourishing woollen industry. The three-mile Convoy bank lay beyond, much of it at 1-in-50, followed by a descent equally severe into Glenmaquin, a place equidistant between Raphoe and Letterkenny and formerly an ETS station with a crossing loop. The remaining five miles into Letterkenny were practically all on a down grade, at 1-in-50 or thereabouts. The Londonderry & Lough Swilly line was crossed about a mile before the terminus, and nearby a branch ran off to a pier, once the terminus for a steamer service down Lough Swilly.

The County Donegal and Lough Swilly stations were side by side at Letterkenny, and the two systems were connected by a spur line. After the Swilly had ceased to run trains, this spur line was left in position, enabling wagons to be run into their goods yard and to be off-loaded into L & LS road vehicles.

The Londonderry trains could use either face of Strabane's island platform. Gaining height on an embankment, the line crossed the Great Northern's route to Derry and traversed the valley to its east side. That side of the Foyle was marshy and offered no inducement for track construction or for subsequent traffic. Instead, the line struck north-east towards the tributary valley of the Burn Dennet. Ballymagorry Halt served the small village of that name, and also nearby Artigarvan. Just after crossing the Burn Dennet, Donemana station was entered, 68 ft above sea level.

The line then began a climb towards a range of low hills, covering three miles, mostly at 1-in-80, to Cullion Halt, and then continuing to the summit at 217 ft, at Desertone, two miles away from the bank of the Foyle. The descent towards the riverside was steep and winding, falling for 1¼ miles at 1-in-83, slackening slightly to

1-in-99 into Newbuildings, and then dropping away again for a mile and a half towards the woods of Prehen House and the river bank. Across the Foyle, a third of a mile away, was the Great Northern line, and the two kept in company on a water-level route into the city of Derry.

ACCIDENTS

The early years of the system were remarkably free of accidents. The first which merits chronicling was spectacular rather than serious, and took place on the West Donegal on 29 January 1884 as a result of stormy weather. A westerly gale driving down from the mountains blew part of the 5.55 p.m. mixed train from Stranorlar to Druminin off the rails 130 yd from Stranorlar station platform. The train consisted of the engine, running chimney first, a covered wagon, one of the two composite carriages and a brake van. Samuel Bingham was driving. The three vehicles were lifted bodily off the track and fell to the inside of the curve. The carriage rested on the edge of the upper step, the lower one being broken away. Where the derailment occurred the train was on a curving embankment, and approaching the high girder bridge spanning the River Finn. Had it reached the bridge the results would have indeed been serious but, as it was, none of the eight passengers was any the worse. The Stranorlar staff took measures to prop up the vehicles, and traffic was resumed the next day when the wind had died down and the line was cleared.

Examination of the track after the accident showed that the outer rail of the curve had 4½ in. of super-elevation, and this was regarded by Major-General Hutchinson, inspecting for the Board of Trade, as a contributory factor. Since speed was never high there, he recommended that the super-elevation be reduced to around one inch.

It is interesting to note that 12 minutes after the Stranorlar accident, a Londonderry & Lough Swilly train suffered a similar fate when approaching Letterkenny from Tooban. The official reports on both these accidents emphasised that the carriages were long and therefore were comparatively unstable in a strong side wind. It was recommended that future carriages should not be longer than 18 ft, though this advice was never actually followed.

A tragic accident occurred on 25 October 1905 on the 3.15 p.m. train running from Londonderry to Strabane, and resulted in the death of the driver, Patrick Tyrrell. Apparently he had been leaning from the cab and looking towards the rear of his train but failed to notice an approaching overbridge. His head struck the masonry, he was thrown from the engine and died at once. The fireman, Manus Grant, halted the train and then brought it into Strabane. It so happened that the general manager was there, and no other driver being available, Livesey drove the train on to Stranorlar, and afterwards took out the 6.10 p.m. to Killybegs, stayed there overnight and drove the 8.35 a.m. up to Stranorlar the next day.

The next serious accident was again on the Derry line, on Sunday, 7 September 1913, at Donemana, the only intermediate passing loop on the Londonderry branch. The Sunday train service consisted merely of a morning train to Londonderry, which returned in the late evening to Strabane. In the interim, the train crew were expected to occupy themselves in Londonderry as best they could. Neil Fullerton was the driver and William Doherty his fireman. After the accident they stated that their time in the city had been spent resting and reading, and eating a hearty Sunday lunch at the house of another railway employee. Contrary evidence was brought, however, to show that they left Derry intoxicated. Leaving Derry at 9.0 p.m. with a train of five coaches, headed by No. 19 *Letterkenny*, they managed the six miles to Cullion without incident, but then took the bit in their teeth on the downhill bank to Donemana. A speed limit of 6 m.p.h. was in force at the loop there, but it was estimated that they entered it at around 40 m.p.h. The engine and the first two carriages (Nos. 51 and 52) left the rails and fell on their sides. The three coaches following (Nos. 20, 5 and 15) remained on the rails. One passenger was killed and another seriously injured. Criminal proceedings were taken; Fullerton received four months' imprisonment with hard labour, but Doherty was discharged.

The vicinity of Strabane station witnessed two accidents in 1916, both of which involved trains working on the Londonderry branch. On 3 March, the 3.5 p.m. Londonderry—Strabane mixed train became derailed at 3.48 p.m. at the Canal overbridge near Strabane. The train was made up of locomotive No. 10 *Sir James*, two wagons and three bogey carriages (Nos. 13, 26 and 46). A broken spring shoe on the second wagon, which contained manure, caused it to derail and eventually the whole train came off the line. The parapet of the bridge prevented the vehicles from running down the embankment, but much damage was done to them, and four persons were injured. A horse was killed in the leading wagon. The leading carriage had its body torn off the frame, and the second carriage was partly telescoped.

On 22 July 1916, as the 8.28 p.m. train was leaving the loop siding for Londonderry, through a lapse on the part of the signalman the trailing bogey of one coach was derailed, and the goods wagon following. Both vehicles were thrown on their sides on the diamond crossing. Of the six passengers in the coach, two were visibly injured, but all six claimed compensation. This was paid, and varied from £60 to £125.

More serious than any of the preceding was a collision between railcar 17 and the engine of a goods train on 29 August 1949. The 2.10 p.m. railcar had left Donegal for Ballyshannon, without the driver having the staff for the section. Half a mile from Donegal, where the line curved southwards in a leafy cutting, the railcar rammed locomotive No. 10 *Owenea*, which was hauling a special Ballyshannon—Donegal goods. The smoke-box of the engine was driven through the railcar's driving cabin and into the passenger compartment beyond. The railcar driver, James McIntyre, was killed instantly, and two women passengers died soon afterwards. Others in the railcar were injured. The Government inquiry showed that the primary cause of the accident was McIntyre's carelessness or forgetfulness in not having the staff in his possession. Criticism was made of slackness on the part of the Donegal station staff in not clearly informing the railcar driver that a special goods was approaching, and in permitting railcars to leave without a clear starting signal from competent station personnel.

A spectacular derailment took place on 23 November 1951 in the townland of Bonagee, near milepost 17½, between one and two miles out of Letterkenny. Driver W. McFeely and Fireman J. Doherty were on the 2—6—4 tank engine *Blanche*, with 16 covered wagons and a guard's van behind them. They had left Strabane at 9.17. On the falling gradient approaching Letterkenny, the train was running a trifle fast, and eight wagons and the van derailed. An underbridge over a secondary road was a short distance ahead. The flailing wagons struck the parapet wall of the bridge, and one of them mounted it and fell 30 ft to the road below. The wagon was full of bags of sugar. Wagon and contents burst on impact. Sugar in the dry state is pleasant stuff, but seven tons after exposure to the rains of a Donegal winter were not to the liking of the break-down personnel. They were ankle-deep in the sticky stuff. The guard's van following the eight wagons was fortunately prevented from falling by lodging against the bridge parapet. Five hundred yards of permanent way were torn up, and wagons 184 and 327 were destroyed.

In those later days, derailments were not unknown, and their incidence reflected the deterioration of the permanent way. Drivers were skilled at minimising the incidents. As a certain senior driver has told:

> I was coming through the Gap and I had Tommy McNulty firing to me. I had a bus and several wagons. One of the wagons went off and I saw her myself going off. It was out the length of the chains. Tommy says to me 'There's a wagon off'. 'I know it, I'm just watching her.' I had shut her off at the time. It was after I came through Derg Bridge. There was a hollow in the road and I was watching back at the train. If I had got her going, and all the buffers like that I knew I was quite safe, but if I saw one of them swinging I knew for to reach for the regulator to shut her off. Tommy says 'Brake her'. 'No,' I says, 'if I brake her the whole thing's up into the field.' So I ran for a mile and a half and whenever I got stopped I had only to put in a jack to put her on—half an hour's work.

Runaways were also known. There was one that involved one of the pioneer diesel railcars, either No. 7 or No. 8. It was before they had the vacuum brakes and as was the usual custom after overhaul, George Brooks the fitter took the car out towards the Gap as far as Lough Mourne. Coming back down, and running backwards, George found that the brakes were not working, and tried in vain to slow the car with a floorboard, pushed through an inspection hole against a wheel. As luck had it, he had a clear road, but he went through Stranorlar and did not get stopped until he was some way down the Finn Valley line. The story goes that he then drove back to Stranorlar, where Henry was waiting on the platform to greet him.

One of the August Bank Holiday specials did its best to behave similarly. The engine was *Blanche* and she had brought 13 carriages and 1,000 people back from Ballyshannon, and up through the Gap. The old brake pipes weren't in too good order after lying out in the weather for months. The driver happened to be one of those who knew it all, and even the presence in the cab of the locomotive inspector didn't curb him. On the falling gradient after Lough Mourne the train began to pick up speed, and before the driver knew, she was away on him. The inspector hastily assumed command, and applied panic measures. Leading sanders on, reverse gear and full regulator! 'The wheels weren't locked, they couldn't lock, she was going the wrong road and she was putting up lumps of coal the size of your fist,' as he told the story 12 years later. The train was booked to stop at Meenglas. They got her halted a quarter of a mile beyond it, but that was better than raking round the curves and into Stranorlar. Brought to a halt, a carriage door opened and two active, if elderly ladies dropped lightly to the ballast. They walked towards the engine and, passing it, called up to the crew 'Thank you, you've saved us a walk—that's our house up there'. They didn't know how lucky they were.

Finally, one must mention an incident in the grey dawn of a winter morning in 1934. It was about 9 a.m. on 31 January and as the 8.10 a.m. railcar from Ballyshannon was within a mile of Donegal station, it ran over and killed a donkey which had strayed on to the railway through an open accommodation gate. The railcar was undamaged. The driver explained that in the distance he mistook the donkey for a railway ganger walking the line and when he discovered his mistake he was too close, and was unable to pull up in time.

Page 143: STRANORLAR—2

(above) Railcar No. 7 at main platform. Note the bookstall; (below) The exterior of the FVR headquarters and office block

Page 144: BRIDGES

*(above) Urney bridge, Finn Valley section; (below) River Foyle bridge
between Strabane and Lifford, on the S & L section*

CHAPTER VII

Motive Power and Rolling Stock

STEAM LOCOMOTIVES

A total of 23 steam locomotives belonged to the owning companies. Three were purchased by the WDR, twelve by the DR, and eight by the CDRJC.

Table 3 lists the engines and shows their division into six classes. Table 4 gives details of the dimensions applicable to each class, and these are amplified in the accompanying sketches.

The average age of the engines when withdrawn from service was 43 years, four had the shortest span of 31 years, while after 56 years one was still working when the line closed.

The practice of carrying both numbers and names was begun by the West Donegal, and was continued throughout the life of the system.

In Class 1, the three Sharp Stewart 2—4—0 tanks *Alice, Blanche* and *Lydia* were not all named, as has been stated elsewhere, after the daughters of the 4th Viscount Lifford. Lord Lifford married twice, and had in fact six daughters, only one of whom, Alice, enjoyed the privilege of seeing her name cast in brass and carried on an engine. Blanche was the wife of Lord Lifford's third son. Lydia was the name of the 4th Viscount's second wife, who was Alice's mother.

While they worked between Stranorlar and Druminin, the annual mileage of the West Donegal engines was about 7,000. No. 1 *Alice* was lent to the Cork, Blackrock & Passage Railway for three years. She seems to have been popular with the southern enginemen, for during 1920 letters were exchanged between Cork and Stranorlar over her possible purchase. Nos. 2 and 3 had been scrapped eight years before, she was the last of her line, and the Cork men were probably hopeful of a bargain. They offered £400, a not unreasonable sum considering her age, but the Joint Committee turned this down. In January 1921, it was reported that *Alice* had suffered serious damage in the hands of the CB & P, and

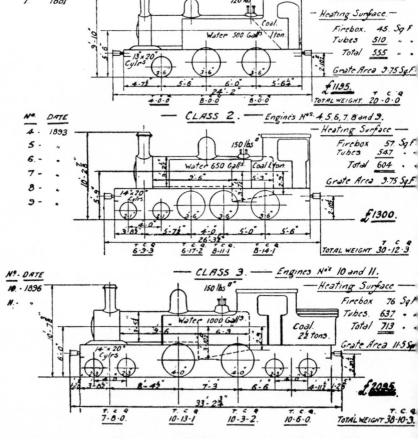

Dimensioned sketches of steam locomotives, Classes 1, 2 & 3,
from the private notebook of G. T. Glover

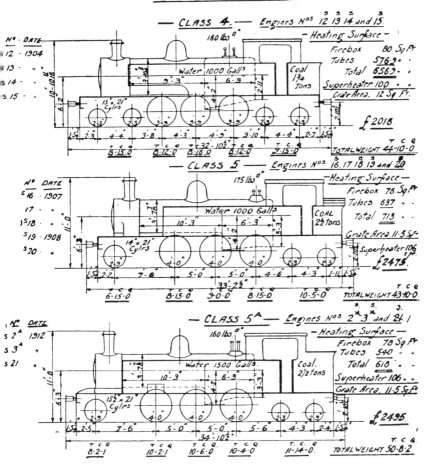

Dimensioned sketches of steam locomotives, Classes 4, 5 and 5A,
from the private notebook of G. T. Glover.

the repairs cost £375 9s 8d. By September 1921, the deal was definitely off, and *Alice* was returned to Donegal. Though she is reputed to have spent the next five years shunting at Stranorlar, G. T. Glover's notes credit her with no mileage then, and it seems unlikely that she was used. Her mileage on the CB & PR totalled 27,763 made up as follows: 1918 (8 months)—7,099 miles, 1919— 16,073 miles, 1920—3,737 miles, 1921—854 miles.

No. 2 *Blanche* and No. 3 *Lydia* were out of service from 1905 and were broken up in 1909 and 1910 respectively. The water and coal capacity of the Class 1 engines was small, but it was sufficient while the line only extended to Donegal. At a later date a steel sheet was wedged over the firebox casing, thus providing additional coal-carrying capacity on top of the tank.

The engines of Class 2, six 4—6—0 tanks built in Glasgow by Neilson, were the forerunners of what was to become a popular type of engine on the Irish narrow gauge, for four rather similar engines were made for the Letterkenny & Burtonport Extension and five for the West Clare. The names *Meenglas* and *Drumboe* on Nos. 4 and 5 were taken from the residences of Lord Lifford and Sir Samuel Hayes, Bt. *Inver* was a village between Donegal and Killybegs. *Finn* and *Foyle* were rivers touched by the system, and *Columbkille* was no doubt drawn from the village of Glencolumb-kille, remotely set on the coast 15 miles north-west of Killybegs.

Water and coal capacity of the Class 2 engines was little different from those of Class 1. The coal was carried in small side bunkers, behind the tanks and flanking the firebox, and it was only sufficient for 60 to 70 miles running. The bearings of the driving wheels were outside, while those of the bogies were inside.

The available records of Class 2 engine mileages cover 1913 to 1927 or 1931. Over that period, fluctuations in totals per annum reflect periodic shoppings and the energetic use of this class during the early 1920s.

No.	Maximum annual miles	Average annual miles	Major overhauls
4	31,533 (1924)	10,831 (1913-31)	1923, 1927
5	22,641 (1922)	11,906 (1913-27)	1924
6	30,238 (1923)	13,199 (1913-27)	1914, 1922
7	27,770 (1922)	13,189 (1913-27)	1924
8	23,429 (1922)	9,869 (1913-31)	1918
9	31,302 (1924)	14,521 (1913-31)	1922

Nos. 5, 6 and 7 were withdrawn during 1927, but were not

scrapped until 1931. No. 4 survived them by four years. Nos. 8 and 9 lasted until 1937.

The two Class 3 engines were the only examples of the 4—4—4 wheel arrangement on any Irish railway. R. M. Livesey has stated that the larger driving wheels, 4 ft in diameter against the 3 ft 6 in. of Classes 1 and 2, were adopted for fast passenger work between Stranorlar and Derry. They were built by Neilson, Reid of Glasgow two years after the opening of the Derry road. While they probably suited fast running, it is surprising that Livesey returned to the four-coupled layout, which gave an adhesive weight that was much less than the Class 2 engines, and an axle loading of between 10 and 11 tons, a figure so high that they had had to be restricted for some years to the Stranorlar-Derry section where the rails were heavier. The names of Nos. 10 and 11 were derived from two members of the Board of Directors : Sir James Musgrave and Sir Samuel Hercules Hayes Bt.

The engines of Classes 1, 2 and 3 had ordinary slide valves and Stephenson valve gear, and they were unsuperheated.

The average annual mileage between 1913 and 1931 of Nos. 10 and 11 was 13,914 and 15,204. Maxima were respectively 27,124 and 29,019, both during 1913. Repairs to No. 10 included boiler and firebox work between August and October 1914, when second-hand brass tubes were fitted, and the engine was repainted. Then between August 1920 and January 1921 she was again taken off for heavy repairs, which included the withdrawal of the brass tubes and their replacement with new steel ones, and the fitting of a new cast-iron funnel. No. 11 had a heavy overhaul between June and September 1916. On 2 December 1918 she broke her r.h. driving axle on the Glenties branch, and this afforded opportunity for a heavy overhaul which was due in any case. This extended from January to June 1919, and the inactivity reduced No. 11's mileage during that year to 6,329. The new driving axle was pressed into the wheels by the Great Northern at Dundalk.

The growth of freight traffic on the system brought in the four Baltic-type tanks of Class 4 in 1904. They came from Nasmyth, Wilson's Manchester works, as did all succeeding engines, and they were named *Eske*, *Owenea*, *Erne* and *Mourne*, after rivers in the district. They were the only 4—6—4 engines among the 144 that worked on the narrow-gauge lines of Ireland. Belpaire fireboxes were fitted, with balanced valves, Stephenson gear and rocking shafts. Their total weight of 44½ tons represented a considerable advance on earlier Donegal engines, but the return to six-coupled wheels kept the axle load to a maximum of 8 tons 16 cwt. They were capable of hauling heavy trains, but had a reputation of being poor steamers and of being extravagant in coal. Due to their rather high axle load they were restricted to the Stranorlar-Derry section until 1907, after which, with the replacement of 45 lb rails with 60 lb, they were free to work over the entire system. As supplied, they were not superheated, but Livesey superheaters were fitted at various dates between 1921 and 1933.

The Baltic's heating surface totalled 723 sq. ft in the unsuperheated state, made up of 80 sq. ft firebox and 643 sq. ft tubes. Superheating raised the total heating surface to 757 sq. ft, in which the firebox was as before, but the tube area was reduced to 577 sq. ft and the superheater added 100 sq. ft.

The mileage statistics of the Baltic engines between 1913 and 1931 were noted by G. T. Glover:

No.	Maximum annual miles	Average annual miles	Major overhauls
12	29,563 (1929)	15,959 (1913-31)	1916, 1921
13	36,070 (1924)	12,610 (1913-17, 1922-31)	1915, 1922
14	25,162 (1928)	14,637 (1913-31)	1914, 1918
15	33,287 (1926)	14,642 (1913-31)	1921

Compared with the engines of the later classes (5 and 5A), the Baltics ran lower mileages for much of their working lives. No. 13 in particular seems to have been in the nature of a standby, for over the five years 1913-17 she only ran up 25,000 miles, and then lay out of use until 1921. Then after a heavy overhaul which took from November 1921 until November 1922, she covered 1,806 miles in eight weeks and went on to surpass her sisters in 1923 by covering 22,448 miles. Her 36,070 miles in 1924 was the highest of any Baltic over the available span of years. The Baltics were numbered 12 to 15 at first. By 1937, vacant numbers left by the Classes 2 and 3 scrappings were filled, the four engines becoming Nos. 9, 10, 11 and 12.

The five 2—6—4 tank engines of Class 5, bought in 1907-8, could do the work of the Baltics, but they steamed better and according to Livesey, used 6 lb/mile less coal, though this is not reflected in 1913-31 coal usage figures. The wheel bearings were all outside. Livesey states that this class was based on the 4—4—4 engines of Class 3. According to him 'the same boiler was used' and the fact that identical heating surfaces have been given for the two, has led to the acceptance of this statement. But a critical examination of the available data by Messrs P. Mallon and R. N. Clements, kindly communicated to the writer, challenges Livesey's notion.

Reference to the diagrams shows that, though Class 3 was followed in the reversion to a round-top firebox, the boiler barrels of Classes 3 and 5 differed greatly in both diameter and length, and that the Class 5 firebox was much deeper than the Class 3, though the length was the same. Errors in diagrams, or incredible coincidence? A study shows that there was in fact one slight error—the original general arrangement of Class 3 shows 75 instead of 76 sq. ft in the firebox, but the rest was coincidence. As it obviously must have, the deepening of the firebox in Class 5 considerably increased the heating surface, but all but 1 sq. ft of the increase was lost by narrowing the crown of the box (and so the upper parts of both tubeplates) by nearly 3 in. The narrower tubeplates involved a reduction in the number of tubes, and Class 5 had only 132 against 142 in Class 3, but this was strictly balanced by the increase of 9 in. in length, both figures of 637 sq. ft being correct. It is hard to follow the reason for the narrow firebox crown of Class 5, considering the increase in boiler diameter of $2\frac{3}{8}$ in., and in fact Class 5A reverted to the firebox with the wider crown. It can be noted from the diagram that these boxes are identical in elevation with those of Class 5, but are shown with an extra 2 sq. ft of heating surface.

Class 5 engines were originally saturated and their total heating surface was, as we have seen, 76 + 637 sq. ft. With the exception of No. 17, they were given Livesey superheaters as they came through the shops during the 1920s (Nos. 16, 18, 19 and 20 in 1926, 1925, 1929 and 1924 respectively) and the heating surface then measured 76 + 503 + 106 sq. ft. The original boiler tubes were brass, but during heavy overhauls during the first war they were given steel tubes, though No. 19 in early 1915 emerged from the shops with 127 new steel and 5 second-hand brass tubes. They had Walschaerts valve gear with balanced slide valves.

The Class 5 engines were at first named after towns served by the railway, and *Donegal*, *Glenties*, *Killybegs*, *Letterkenny* and *Raphoe* were allocated to Nos. 16, 17, 18, 19 and 20 respectively. As already noted, the six Class 2 engines were scrapped between 1931 and 1937, and after the last of them was gone, five of their plates were used to rename Class 5. Concurrently, the class was renumbered. So *Meenglas*, *Drumboe*, *Finn* and *Foyle* retained their Class 2 numbers, but *Columbkille* exchanged 9 for 6. The name *Inver* was not used again. The 1913-31 mileage statistics for the Class 5 engines overleaf reflect their success in higher mileages than any earlier engines.

No.	Maximum annual mileage	Average annual mileage
16/4	39,194 (1916)	23,062
17/5	36,439 (1930)	19,023
18/6	33,468 (1927)	22,092
19/7	28,167 (1914)	18,925
20/8	29,533 (1924)	19,351

During the first war these engines were worked really hard with shoppings for heavy overhauls as much as 60,000 miles apart. As a result of this hard use, their coal consumption rose markedly and was highest in 1919, when No. 6 used 51.7 lb/mile and No. 20 52.5 lb/mile. Improved maintenance in the 1920s greatly improved matters: in 1923 No. 20 is credited with the remarkable figure of 25 lb/mile, but as she only ran 2,988 miles then, the figure is probably not representative. No. 19's score of 29.5 to 33 lb/mile over the six years 1925-30 is about the steadiest on record.

On the Class 3, 4 and 5 engines, the maximum amount of water carried was 1,000 gallons, but under the Joint Committee plans were put forward for a new class of engine that would have 2,000 gallon tanks. Nasmyth, Wilson suggested that by fitting Schmidt super-heaters the tanks could be reduced to 1,500 gallons and, since this reduced weight, it was adopted. Of the total, 200 gallons was held in a small bunker tank, illustrated in Livesey's 1912 description. This was later removed, reducing the tanks to 1,300 gallons, but increasing the coal capacity by 13 cwt. Initially, the new engines were meant to be duplicates of Class 5 apart from the altered tanks, but the addition of superheaters, larger bore cylinders and piston valves, resulted in them being placed in Class 5A. Other features, which made their design the most advanced of any Irish narrow-gauge engine, were the use of Wakefield's mechanical lubricators for cylinders and valves, forced lubrication for all axle journals and bogie centres, Boyer speed indicator, smoke-box ash ejector and variable blast-pipe. At first they were numbered 21, 2A and 3A, the 'A' suffix to the numbers recalling the Great Northern practice that was in vogue up to 1913 of numbering old 'duplicate' engines. But it is difficult to see why this should have been done to the two Class 5A engines, since the original 2 and 3 had been scrapped some years before. However, they appear from the official engine repair records to have carried the 'A' until 1917, after which they were noted as Nos. 2 and 3. No. 21 became No. 1 during 1927. The three engines, at first *Ballyshannon*, *Strabane* and *Stranorlar*, continued the Class 5 practice of being named after towns on the railway, but they eventually took the names of the Class 1 engines; the changes probably became effective during visits to the shops about 1927-30.

By 1937, withdrawals had left only engines of Classes 4, 5 and 5A in use; from then until the end, 21 years later, representatives of each of these three classes remained at work.

The haulage capacity of the engines, given in the Working Time Tables, shows some variation between 1911 and 1913, suggesting that Forbes was still formulating the optimum load. Thus in May 1911, No. 1 *Alice* was listed at a limit of 70 tons over all the system, and a supplementary note stated that this engine usually worked the 4.40 p.m. Stranorlar-Glenties and 6.20 p.m. Glenties-Stranorlar trains, its haulage capacity was limited and the Stranorlar Agent was to see that every effort was made to lighten the 4.40 p.m. train by utilising the two earlier trains.

A more detailed statement of engine haulage capacity was given in the Working Time Table for July 1914, by which time the Class 5A engines had proved themselves:

Section of Line	Class of Engine					
	1	2	3	4	5	5A
	tons	tons	tons	tons	tons	tons
Derry—Strabane	130	190	165	225	200	230
Strabane—Letterkenny	95	130	135	160	145	165
Letterkenny—Strabane	100	135	120	165	150	170
Strabane—Stranorlar	255	375	325	445	400	450
Stranorlar—Glenties	100	140	145	200	180	205
Glenties—Stranorlar	100	140	130	175	155	180
Stranorlar—Donegal	100	140	140	175	155	180
Donegal—Ballyshannon	105	150	130	180	160	185
Ballyshannon—Donegal	115	170	145	200	180	205
Donegal—Killybegs	85	125	110	145	130	150
Killybegs—Donegal	90	125	120	155	145	160

The loads were regulated by the gross weight and the latter was calculated on the following basis:

	Empty	Loaded
Passenger carriage or van	11 tons	14 tons
Open wagons	4 tons	11 tons
Covered goods or cattle wagons	4¼ tons	11 tons

Until 1906 the engine livery was green, with black bands and white lines. From 1906 until about 1937, it was black, lined red. After 1937, an attractive geranium red was adopted; this was either unlined, or lined out in white (and possibly also in yellow).

Engine nameplates were cast in brass, with a raised edge, and were affixed in the middle of the side tanks. Those of *Alice, Blanche* and *Lydia* had seriffed letters, those of the other engines had the names in block capitals.

Engine numbers were first given as No. 1, up to Class 3, and were painted or transferred on to the side tanks, behind the nameplates in Class 1, and below the nameplates in the other classes. At a later date, the prefix 'No.' was left out. Classes 4, 5 and 5A were given cast brass numberplates when built, and these were sited on the cab side-sheets, and rectangular, raised-edge plate bearing the digit only. When the Class 5 engines were renumbered, plates seem to have been cast only for 6 and 8, while 4 and 5 got painted numbers. When 2A and 3A were renumbered, new plates were not cast, but the 'A' was filed off, leaving the digit offset. A new plate was cast for the 21/1 renumbering of *Alice*.

At the system's peak, in 1923, there were seven locomotive sheds in use, housing 10 of the 21 engines, and the distribution of engines and crews is as shown. The single-road shed at Donegal was out of use by then.

Shed	No. of locos.	No. of crews
Derry	1	2
Strabane	2	3
Letterkenny	1	1
Stranorlar	3	4
Glenties	1	2
Ballyshannon	1	2
Killybegs	1	1
Total	10	15
Spare at Stranorlar	5	
Awaiting repair	2	
Under repair	4	
Total stock	21	

RAILCARS

Mention has already been made of the acquisition in 1907 of the first rail motor vehicle. This was a diminutive four-wheeled affair made by Messrs Allday & Onions of Birmingham, and it was bought on the recommendation of R. M. Livesey. It had an open body, and was intended to be used simply as an inspection car. One bench-type seat was placed transversely across the back of the car, a separate front seat was provided for the driver. A partition separated the front and back portions, and would have given the passengers a little protection from the elements. No photographs of the vehicle in this state are known.

In September 1911, shortly after his arrival, Henry Forbes expressed his opinion of the inspection car in a letter to the Committee, saying that 'it was not in use six times during the past year' and was 'not really required for our purposes'. But he kept it nevertheless, and 15 years later had cause to be glad of it, when the coal strike forced him to use it for the carriage of passengers and mails. On 11 November 1926 he wrote a lengthy memorandum, covering over three pages of quarto and headed 'Rail Motor', and said of the 19-year-old vehicle:

It did not come up to expectations, the engine was continually giving trouble, the car was of little real service, and for the most part, was laid up. In 1920 the engine was scrapped and a Ford engine fitted, the original gears and axles being retained; it was also covered in and seated six persons, but even in its altered form was seldom used except for an occasional trip with the Engineers.

In June last the Coal Strike gave us the opportunity we wanted to experiment with it for general purposes; to save coal a steam train between Stranorlar and Glenties was discontinued and its place taken by this rail motor, principally for the carrying of the morning mails. We also used it from Stranorlar to Strabane and back daily, as by doing so we were able to save £4-10-0 a week in Enginemen's overtime by its carrying a relief crew. Gradually passengers came to know of its running and although its normal capacity was six, it usually carried a great deal more, served a useful purpose and allowed us to carry on. For the months of June, July and August this little car ran over 6,000 miles without a single failure.

On 5th September we were unfortunate enough to entrust the driving of it, for an emergency run, to one of our Engine Drivers, a man with over 30 years' experience on the footplate, who had been given instructions in its use. On his very first trip from Stranorlar to Glenties, through rough handling, he completely smashed the gears, and left the car a wreck, and it had to be towed back to Stranorlar. To have special gears cut in England would have meant great delay, and it was decided to refit it with a complete new Ford Axle Assembly, procured from the local Ford dealer, as being the easiest and most satisfactory way out of the difficulty. . . . The alterations were made here at a cost of about £50, including wages and materials. The rough handling by the Engineman let us in for all this extra expense, and the experience we have had confirms the opinion of all Motor experts, that steam drivers or firemen should not be allowed to handle or have anything to do with motor vehicles. While the car was in the shops, the seating was improved; it can now carry ten persons comfortably, and is in perfect order and available at Stranorlar for emergency work.

For the first 19 years of its career this vehicle was variously referred to in the records as the 'railcar', the 'car', the 'motor' or the 'inspection car'. It apparently carried no number; certainly it was not numbered 1 in the railcar series until the arrival of Nos. 2 and 3 in 1926. The original power unit is stated by Forbes to have been of 10 h.p., the 1920 rebuild to which he refers gave it a 22 h.p. Ford engine and in July 1949 it was repowered with a 36 h.p. Ford engine out of Railcar No. 9. These changes were accompanied by alterations in the bonnet, radiator and front suspension.

Internally, the wooden body which it was given in 1920 was 8 ft 5 in. in length and 3 ft 7 in. in width, and there was very little overhang compared with the other railcars. Forbes claimed to seat 'ten persons comfortably' in this space: official drawings show it to have seating for seven persons.

Originally the diameter of the front wheels was 2 ft, and that of the rear wheels 2 ft 6 in., giving the vehicle a slight look of a Manx cat. In January 1930, new 2ft 2in. wheels were fitted front and rear, and probably about this time longitudinal semi-elliptic springs were fitted outside the front wheels.

The necessarily-limited seating prevented any great extension of its use, but increased power in latter years allowed it to haul a trailer on the level Finn Valley section. Up to the end of April 1956 it ran 19,457 miles. It was then withdrawn, and is preserved in the Belfast Transport Museum.

The use of this railcar on the Glenties line transformed Forbes's opinion of its capabilities and did much to shape future policy on the use of railcars. Already wanting something more powerful and roomy, Forbes wrote to G. T. Glover on 11 June 1926:

After a fortnight's practical experience of the small car, with its limited accommodation, I have absolutely satisfied myself that a rail motor of a larger type can be usefully and economically employed for the conveyance of mails and passengers between here and Glenties, during a certain period of each day. A car capable of hauling a few wagons would have suited better, but as this cannot apparently be had, the alternative is to provide a passenger coach capable of carrying a maximum of 20 people with space for mails, newspapers and small parcels with a railing on top for luggage &c. The goods traffic I will arrange to work at certain times with an engine.

My idea would be to get an engine of the Ford lorry type, easily driven, and have it built into chassis at Stranorlar by our own men, with a very light body, preferably aluminium, and fitted with comfortably upholstered seats, as in a bus, attractively painted in artistic colours inside and outside, one class only.

One man only to be employed: the Driver would also issue tickets at Halts and collect them from passengers alighting, and would also require to assist in handling mails, papers and parcels at Stations.

I have figured it out that we could almost pay for the car (the cost alone not to exceed £300) in one year by the savings effected in fuel alone, apart altogether from the reduction in wages. We could give a more efficient service than at present, and at reduced fares.

Having regard to our serious financial position the matter is of urgent importance. . . .

Two courses lay open to Glover, the first to produce a suitable vehicle between the Dundalk and Stranorlar shops, the second to purchase from outside. Advised by his chief draughtsman, L. J. Watson, Glover replied to Forbes on 18 June 1926 that the GNR were prepared to build a railcar:

As you have fixed such a low maximum cost it will be difficult to provide the accommodation you propose, but the Sketch will give you an idea of what we can provide and will enable you to suggest improvements to suit the traffic . . . estimate that we could provide the complete underframe ready for body to be built on to it, for £150 maximum. . . . The body meanwhile could be building at Stranorlar.

Also on 18 June, Glover wrote to W. T. D. Grundy, the general manager of the Derwent Valley Light Railway, whose two 4-ft 8½-in.-gauge railcars were being advertised for sale. Three days later he visited York and inspected the 'Ford Buses'. These railcars had been bought by the DVLR in May 1924 as Ford ton truck chassis, and had been fitted with bodies by C. H. Roe Ltd of Leeds. The pair cost the DVLR £1,070. It was general practice to run them in tandem, back to back, using one of the motors at a time. Glover furnished Forbes with a detailed description on his return and ended by saying:

If you can spare the time it would be worth while a visit on your part as the vehicles are absolutely what you suggest. The only doubtful matter is the overhang on each side over our gauge and I am making a calculation on the subject. There is no doubt that such a large body would catch a side wind severely.

The memory of the serious accident at the Owencarrow Viaduct on the Londonderry & Lough Swilly Railway, in January of the previous year, was clearly in Glover's mind, and he intended to take no risks with his railcars in the winter gales.

Since straightforward regauging of the railcars would have given them a very high centre of gravity, Glover recommended two alternatives: either a complete rebuild of the bodies involving a narrowing from 7 ft to 5 ft 10 in., or else a drastic lowering. The latter course would assist entry from the low Donegal platforms, or from the ground at certain halts, but it would involve some rebuilding to accommodate the rear wheels. In early July, Glover sent Michael Byrne, his carriage shop foreman, to the Layerthorpe station at York, and together they decided that lowering presented no great difficulty.

With Forbes enthusiastically advocating an expansion of railcar traction, formal authorisation was given to purchase the two DVLR cars. Forbes visited York, only to find that Lt. Col. Stephens of the East Kent Railway was also interested. Glover had mentioned a price of £500; Forbes had hoped to cut this by £100, but he was forced to go to £480 to secure them for the CDRJC. For good measure the Derwent Valley Light Railway threw in a new spare engine, auxiliary gearbox and magneto.

The railcars arrived in Derry on 7 August 1926. Since they fitted neither of the Irish gauges, and would have fouled the over-bridges when mounted on flat wagons, their transport overland presented some difficulties. Ultimately they had to be partly dismantled, body and frames being loaded separately.

At Castlefinn the Free State customs officer lay in wait, claiming that they were motor buses and therefore liable to import duty of 33⅓ per cent on the value and freight—in all £166 8s 7d. Forbes held that they were railway vehicles and were therefore exempt from import duty. His furious protests were in vain. The customs officer was prepared to detain them indefinitely, and to get them the further six miles up the Finn Valley the duty was paid. Forbes forthwith applied to the Revenue Commissioners in Dublin for a refund and some time later, to his delight, he obtained it.

The original intention appears to have been to alter the bodies of the two railcars at Stranorlar, and the frames and axles at Dundalk. Work had in fact started at Stranorlar, when Glover wrote to Forbes:

> It is quite evident now that the original proposal to lower the body a few inches only will not be safe, and it will be far less expensive and more speedy in the long run to have all the alterations made here, rather than sending the chassis and Foreman Byrne to Stranorlar.

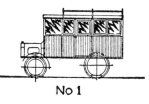

No 1

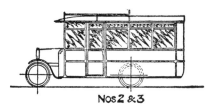

Nos 2 & 3

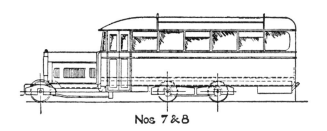

Nos 7 & 8

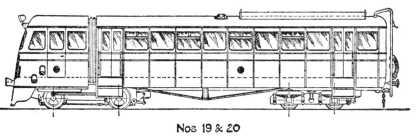

Nos 19 & 20

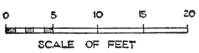

SCALE OF FEET

Petrol and Diesel Railcars

The total cost of conversion came to £128 11s 8d.

The first of the converted railcars was sent from Dundalk to Stranorlar on 7 September, the second followed on 22 October 1926. Numbered 2 and 3, they went into service at once. With their rear wheels nearly concealed by their lowered bodies, they had a peculiar appearance, aptly compared to that of a 'clocking' hen by a certain senior Dundalk engineer.

On 15 November 1926, Forbes wrote to Glover:

> I am very sorry you have been kept so busy, as I would have liked to have seen you about the Motors, which have been doing well; the last one you sent is specially good.
>
> I sent you a report on the working, which I trust will be of interest. . . . [This was his memorandum of 11th November.]
>
> As you will see, the two Motors are now running about 2,400 miles each per month, and we will have to consider what is to be done in the event of their withdrawal for overhaul. I was thinking you might be able to design a light separate coach (without power) on roller or ball bearings, that would accommodate, say, 30 passengers and it could be hauled by the small motor, which I believe it would be quite capable of doing, thus at a moderate cost we would have a combined car for 40 passengers (that is, 10 for the small car and 30 for the coach), which would be a great addition.
>
> I think we should also consider if we could not get the Directors to agree to your designing one or more motors to our own ideas; in the case of one, it would only mean the chassis and bodywork, and rear axle assembly, as we have a spare Ford engine, radiator and Suphaphord*, or as an alternative build a car like No. 1, and another separate coach (without power). Subject to your opinion, it would seem better to have a small driving unit and a separate coach, there would not need to be such a long wheel base, and not the same strain on the rear driving axle; of course, I may be quite wrong in this.
>
> It is evident from the way the Motors are being patronised on this line during the winter, that this form of traction has come to stay, and I anticipate in the summer months we will not be able to meet the demand for them.

At this stage in the development of the railcar services, No. 2 was stabled at Glenties and worked to and from Stranorlar. No. 3 was used both on the Finn Valley and on the Letterkenny sections.

The career of No. 2 and No. 3 was less smooth than old No. 1, for they both developed an unfortunate propensity for breaking their axles. There had been no history of such trouble on the DVLR and severe curves and higher speeds on the Donegal line were blamed. The first accident occurred on 19 November 1926. On the following day, Forbes made his report to Glover:

---

* The Suphaphord was a special 4-speed gearbox.

Page 161 : STRABANE—LETTERKENNY

(above) 0-4-0ST 'Isabella', contractor's locomotive during construction;
(below) Letterkenny station, 5 August 1958. The 11.00 am from Strabane
has arrived on left, consisting of railcar, carriage and van

Page 162: FREIGHT VEHICLES AND 'PHŒNIX'

(above) Timber truck No. 7 *(later renumbered into 309-312 class); (centre)*
Cattle wagon No. 208; *(below)* 'Phœnix', diesel-mechanical tractor No. 11

As the 12.10 p.m. Bus from Stranorlar was running from Ballinamore to Fintown, and on a level part of the road, about ¼ mile from the former station, while travelling at a moderate speed, the Driver heard a loud crack, applied his brakes and immediately after the right hand leading wheel flew off and ran down the slight embankment at the place into the bog below. The bus slightly canted, but did not turn over; all wheels were derailed, and when I arrived it was lying at right angles to the rails. There were five passengers for Glenties, but they did not complain of any injury, and I had them sent by road to destination.

It was found that the axle had snapped close to the hub, where it had been reduced to fit.

We had the greatest difficulty getting the bus on to the rails again, owing to the boggy nature of the ground. We first had to support the front part on a platelayer's bogie; it would not however move in this position, and it was then seen that the rear axle had been damaged, and one of the rear wheels broken, so we had to support the other end on another bogie, and so pushed it into Ballinamore.

A month later Railcar No. 3 misbehaved similarly:

. . . the Rail Motor leaving Stranorlar at 12 noon on 17th inst. was running between Clady and Strabane, when within two miles of the latter station, on a straight part of the road, the *front* axle broke in two places at the wheel hubs, both front wheels flew off, and the front of the Motor dropped on the rails.

There were 15 passengers on the Motor, and the sudden stoppage threw the occupants against one another; one young man—an emigrant—had his lip slightly cut, but I understand caught the steamer at Derry for America; a woman named Wray complained of injury, and an old man, about 60 years of age, named Allen, complained that his leg was injured.

All the passengers were taken to Strabane by road motors, and those injured were able to do their business in Strabane and proceed home by the evening trains. The old man, Allen, has since taken to his bed, and is being attended to by a Doctor.

The only damage to the Motor, as far as can be seen, was the breaking of the front axle—not a pane of glass was broken.

Experience was being obtained in a hard school, Forbes and Glover had no one to guide them, and Forbes was troubled for a time about loss of public confidence in his new railcars. Glover commented: 'It looks as if we must completely strengthen the front end and make the Axles more in accordance with Railway practice'.

On the exposed moorland along the Glenties branch, icy rails gave these two railcars much trouble when on the early-morning mail run, and on at least one occasion it took three hours to get from Stranorlar to Fintown. Forbes opposed using a steam train to clear the night's accumulation of ice on the grounds of cost, and with characteristic ingenuity the Stranorlar men overcame the difficulty by working the two buses coupled together, both engines running and with two drivers. The wheels of the leading car broke the ice film, brushes on the car removed it, and traction was obtained by the second car.

By 1933, Nos. 2 and 3 were wearing out. On 12 May, Forbes wrote to J. B. Stephens, the general manager of the Great Northern, proposing to add to the railcar stock, and saying that Nos. 2 and 3 were 'of an obsolete nature and it is a source of worry to keep them running at all'. By 2 June 1933, in a letter to J. G. Shanahan, the GNR's accountant, Forbes extended his comments, saying '. . . they are in a very bad condition, in fact one is dismantled and it would be money wasted trying to rejuvenate them as they are out of date and most unattractive looking both inside and out'. So the Derwent Valley railcars passed from the Donegal scene, and were officially withdrawn in 1934.

The début of the railcars had been successful, in spite of all their teething troubles, and in 1928 the three pioneers were joined by railcar No. 4. This was based on a 30-cwt Ford chassis, to which the Dundalk works fitted the suspension. The front pair of wheels formed a pony truck, the rear pair were driven through a torque shaft and controlled by a handbrake.

The chassis of No. 4 was delivered at Dundalk at the end of June 1928 and work on the motion was done during July. The van body was meanwhile being built separately by Messrs C. O'Doherty & Son of Strabane. Assembly was completed at Stranorlar, and by early October the railcar was ready. On the 6th of that month, while arranging for Glover to visit Stranorlar to inspect the vehicle, Forbes said: 'O'Doherty has made a fine job of the Bus; it looks remarkably well. I have not been in it yet but Mr. Parks tells me when being hauled up by No. 1 it was extraordinarily steady, and he was greatly surprised; the overhang does not seem to affect it at all and he attributes this to the new class of bearing springs.' It was tested on 16 October 1928 with Glover and Forbes on board. It ran along the Finn Valley section where it reached a maximum speed of 28 m.p.h., and then tackled the bank towards Barnesmore, where it climbed well. So far so good.

Before it was long in service, several disc wheels broke and were replaced with stronger ones. Then on 23 May 1929 a rear axle broke when the railcar was running light from Stranorlar to Strabane. On 5 August 1929, after another similar accident, Forbes wrote to Glover:

I regret to inform you that Rail Motor No. 4 again broke a right hand axle yesterday when returning from Ballyshannon, hauling the trailer. The mishap occurred just as the vehicles were descending the incline at Lough Mourne and the driver was fortunately able to come into Stranorlar by coasting and running very slowly, the wheel remaining in its place. The break occurred just in the same place as before and the sooner we make some change the better . . . as I do not consider it safe to have the car running as it is at present.

A solid rear axle, without differential, was fitted. After some more trouble with broken front stub axles, in mid-1933 these were replaced at Stranorlar with a solid front axle, and the wheelbase was lengthened.

The original body on No. 4 had two doors at the front. Later the offside door was replaced by a rear entrance, reducing the seats from 21 to 20. It was lent for a week to the Clogher Valley Railway for demonstration and test purposes in 1932, before that concern introduced railcars themselves.

Once the difficulties with broken wheels and axles had been overcome, railcar No. 4 gave good service. It lasted throughout World War II, and worked for 19 years before being scrapped.

The estimates for capital expenditure for both 1926 and 1927 list a railcar trailer at £350, and as we have seen, Forbes had put forward active proposals to add in this way to the passenger-hauling capacity of the available railcars. The step was deferred until late in 1928, when in November the Dundalk drawing office made a design for a light passenger-carrying trailer, to run on a 9-ft wheelbase and to be 18 ft 6 in. over the headstocks. Four firms were asked to tender for its construction, but they were not interested in such a small 'one off' job. In the following month it was decided to accept the offer of Knutsford Motors Ltd to make the trailer chassis for £100, and it was delivered in March 1929. The body was put on by O'Doherty at Strabane and the trailer was ready in June in time for the summer services. It was numbered 5 in the railcar series, weighed 3 tons 4½ cwt and seated 28 passengers. Originally it had a roof rack for luggage with access by a rear-end ladder; its lack of buffer or coupling meant that it could not be marshalled in a steam train in emergency. This was overcome in 1938, when Stranorlar works raised the frame; because of the higher roof, luggage could no longer be taken on top, and it was carried in a light, roller-bearing trailer wagon under a tarpaulin. Trailer 5 survived to the end. It was auctioned in March 1961, and became the cash office at the Donegal town football ground.

Railcar No. 6 was, like No. 4, a product of the Great Northern and O'Doherty and began service in 1930. It was considerably more substantial than its progenitors, with an unloaded weight of 5 tons 11 cwt and seats for 30. A 32 h.p. Reo engine was the power unit. It ran on a front radial truck, arranged for side-play of 4½ in. to take the worst curves on the system, and on a rear driving bogie. Normally the drive was only taken to one of the back axles, but both could be chain-coupled in winter to minimise slipping. The chain could be tightened by lengthening the bogie wheelbase. A handbrake was fitted on the rear wheels at first, but vacuum braking was added in November 1931. After 15 years, railcar No. 6 was de-engined and rebuilt as a four-wheeled trailer, with the axles set at 11 ft centres. After its sale in 1958, the body went to a private owner at Invcr.

Nineteen-thirty-one was a memorable year, for then the petrol-engined railcars were joined by the first two diesel-engined vehicles. They were of GNR design, and the underframes were built at Dundalk and given Gardner 6L2 engines. Again O'Doherty built the bodies. No. 7 went into service in June 1931 and was the first diesel-engined railcar to operate regular timetable services in the British Isles. No. 8 joined it in the following November.

The Gardner diesels of Nos. 7 and 8 drove through Thorneycroft 4-speed and reverse gearboxes. Forward ratios were 1, 1.56, 2.75 and 5.13 to 1. The fuel tanks held 23 gallons. The cars were carried on six wheels of 2 ft 2⅜ in. diameter. As the engine and radiator were too wide to allow the front wheels to be below them, the axle of the leading pony truck was placed in front of the radiator and gave the cars a 'sit-up-and-beg' look. The front axle was 14 ft forward of the leading axle of the driving bogie, which had a wheelbase of 5 ft 6 in. and optional chain coupling. A rear-end ladder gave access to a roof rack for light luggage.

The chain on the driving bogie soon caused trouble. It had a long run and, being exposed to wet and dust, it soon wore and stretched. A slapping action developed and breakage followed. A spring-loaded jockey pinion fitted at Stranorlar helped to cure the trouble.

After some seven years' use, complaints were being received that Nos. 7 and 8 railcars were unheated. In February 1937, Forbes asked H. E. Wilson, then chief draughtsman at Dundalk, for his opinion:

> Now that we have No. 7 Railcar in our shops, I was thinking of having it heated as people are beginning to complain of the cold in the winter months when travelling in Nos. 7 and 8 as compared with the others.

> Could you suggest the cheapest method of our doing this: the 'Clayton' is rather costly, and as we have spare pipes here, it would probably be satisfactory if heated from the radiator. I suppose you have nothing surplus we could use up?

Always to the rescue, Dundalk was able to turn up something suitable:

> I find we have on hand 30 cast-iron floor radiators which we removed from Road Buses. These we could let you have for 2/6d each plus carriage. Probably you would require six per car.

Railcars 6, 7 and 8 were employed on the Ballyshannon branch for much of their lives. Occasionally they ran coupled in pairs, with two drivers. In this way they could assist in light goods haulage and could haul as many as eight wagons, though the passengers found the inevitable lack of synchronisation unpleasant when getting away.

Two of the four second-hand road buses bought in 1930, which had run for three years over the rough roads of west Donegal, received a fresh lease of life in 1933. They were rebuilt at Stranorlar and continued their existence as railcars.

As early as August 1932 the germ of the conversion was in Forbes's mind, when he wrote to Glover:

> When you are here on Wednesday next, I would like to consult you as to converting two of our old road buses into one 2-axle trailer seating about 40 passengers, that is if the wheelbase could be extended to a greater extent than in No. 5 Trailer which is 9 feet.
>
> We have a large quantity of long angle irons and plates off the Bridge at Strabane and there would be no difficulty in our putting together the chassis, while we have all the timber, sheeting, glass and seats needed for the body in stock.
>
> We need a vehicle like this for use with Nos. 4 and 6, which would obviate our using Nos. 2 and 3 as Trailers; the latter are now very disreputable looking.

Forbes's enthusiasm, and his confidence in the ability of his own shopmen, was tempered somewhat by Dundalk's knowledge of carriage building. The idea of a composite body built up from two old buses was shelved, and after Dundalk had produced a scheme, Stranorlar got to work and the products emerged on the 3-ft-gauge as railcars No. 9 and No. 10, both very similar in looks to No. 4, and powered by 36 h.p. Ford petrol engines. Twenty passengers could be carried in each car. No. 9 ran for 16 years, but the life of No. 10 was cut short on 27 August 1939 by an accidental fire which destroyed it as it lay in the Ballyshannon shed, locked up after the day's work.

Forty-five miles south-east of Stranorlar, the Clogher Valley Railway Company had taken delivery of an Atkinson-Walker four-wheeled steam tractor. It was fortunate for the CVR that provision had been made with the builders that if the tractor was not success-ful it was to be taken back free of cost. It arrived at Aughnacloy in January 1929 and was a failure from the start. By October its worthlessness had been demonstrated conclusively, but by then the makers had gone bankrupt and were in the hands of a receiver. About this time the direction of the CVR was put in the hands of a Committee of Management, one of the members being Henry Forbes. Being on the spot, as it were, Forbes visualised the poten-tialities of the tractor as a modified unit, and he was advised by Glover that a diesel engine could be fitted. So Forbes set out to buy the body, transmission and frame as cheaply as he could, and after a little bargaining, he purchased the vehicle for 100 guineas. The chassis was sent from Tynan to Dundalk on 19 February 1932, a Gardner 6L2 diesel engine was installed, and after eight months of work it was returned to Stranorlar.

The tractor was ready for trial at the end of December 1932. Diesel oil and cooling water were contained in the side tanks, and it was numbered 11 in the railcar stock. The number was painted on the cab at first, later it acquired the luxury of a cast brass number plate. Because of its resurrection, Forbes named it *Phoenix*, the title being painted in large sans-serif capitals on the side tanks. To give audible warning, a rubber-bulb horn was carried. The engine exhaust was at first taken above roof level by a short stub pipe, later a silencer and fishtail were fixed horizontally on the roof, detracting from the already unbeautiful appearance of *Phoenix*. Although the trial runs in January 1923 were rather disappointing, for it was slow and very noisy in reverse gear, the conversion was in general a success.

In a letter to J. G. Shanahan of the Great Northern, dated 2 June 1933, Forbes gave a survey of the first half-year's working:

> The reasons why I do not think another of our locomotives should be scrapped (other than the two I have already recommended for scrapping) as against the Tractor are that the latter, on account of its limited tractive effort*, is not able to do the same service as a Steam Locomotive, and is really used for speeding up our passenger trains and doing away with the vexatious delays at Customs Stations. It is therefore employed here for light shunting, proceeding to Lifford to propel wagons cleared by the Customs from the main line to

* The tractive effort was only 1,028 lb. when running in top gear at 27 m.p.h.

Ballindrait sidings, returning to Strabane and thence to Castlefinn Customs Station where it shunts and assembles wagons in Station order so as to relieve the following steam train of the delay that formerly took place.

During its period of use, which was up to the end of rail working, *Phoenix II* built up a total of 204,577 miles to its credit. After being used to lift the southern part of the s & l section during 1960, it was moved to the Belfast Transport Museum.

Acquisitions to the railcar stock during 1934 included both new and second-hand vehicles. Railcar 12 came as new stock and was the outcome of design work at Dundalk. It was the first of the Donegal railcars to have a four-coupled power bogie, with the wheels coupled by side rods. The power bogie was sited at the front of the railcar and carried the 6L2 Gardner diesel engine, driving cab and 40-gallon fuel tank. The coach body, built at the Great Northern body shops, was articulated to the power bogie and its weight was also taken on a rear bogie. No. 12's power bogie was built by Walker Bros of Wigan at a cost of £1,308. It was shipped from Heysham and arrived in Londonderry on 22 February 1934, whence it was driven under its own power to Strabane the same evening. The body arrived at Strabane on the following day, and on 24 February the two portions were fitted together to produce the railcar. The overall length was 42 ft 3 in., of which the body accounted for 31 ft 11 in. The total cost of the railcar was £2,281, and with seating accommodation for 41 passengers, it represented a considerable advance in both capacity and design on its fore-runners. It lasted until the 1959 closures, having covered 945,600 miles over its active life of a quarter-century.

The second-hand acquisitions in 1934 came from two sources: the Dublin & Blessington Steam Tramway, which operated south-west of Dublin on a gauge of 5 ft 3 in., and the Castlederg & Victoria Bridge Tramway, which ran on a 3-ft-gauge roadside track in County Tyrone, more or less parallel to the Finn Valley section but some seven miles to the south. Road competition had forced these two concerns to close down in 1932 and 1933 respectively, and in due course their rolling stock came up for auction.

Two vehicles came from the Dublin & Blessington, who since the mid-twenties had been supplementing steam traction by railcars. At the closure, its track and entire rolling stock had been bought by the Hammond Lane Metal Co., who resold two cars to the

Donegal. The smaller was a 22-h.p. Ford-engined railcar of which the D & BST had two. One of them was bought by the Committee, taken to Stranorlar, and operated upon. It continued its existence as a four-wheeled trailer, No. 13, with seats for 16 passengers. After ten years in Donegal, Forbes reported to Dundalk that it was 'now in a rather advanced state of dilapidation', and it was forthwith scrapped.

The Donegal also bought the D & BST's larger railcar, a Drewry 35 h.p. petrol-engined vehicle. It was carried on eight wheels and power was transmitted to the centre pair of axles. As it could be driven from either end, it did not need to be turned at the end of a run. Stranorlar regauged it, and moved the radiator to the roof. It became the second No. 3 railcar, running with 40 seats. After nine years it was rebuilt as a trailer, and thus modified, it saw service until the end, and was then moved to the Belfast Transport Museum.

The second-hand Castlederg & Victoria Bridge Tramway vehicle began its career as a four-coupled railcar in 1925, when it was built in the company's workshop to the design of the locomotive superintendent George H. Pollard. It was powered by a 20 h.p. Fordson engine which ran on paraffin, and held 24 passengers. In spite of being rather underpowered it covered around 30,000 miles over the eight-mile tramway before it was withdrawn in December 1928. It then lay out of use for four years, during which time the engine was taken out and sold to a local sawmill. On 15 December 1932 Henry Forbes viewed the derelict remains and he wrote to G. T. Glover at Dundalk:

> I went today with Mr Armstrong to Castlederg to see the derelict rail motor on hand there. It is certainly not very prepossessing looking as it lies in the scrap heap; the body is of course quite hopeless but the chassis seems to be in fair order with good wheels and axles, fitted with roller bearings, and I think when fitted with a new body would suit us as a trailer. . . . I think a fair offer for it would be £25 or £30 on rail at Victoria Bridge station.

The lower figure was offered, and brought a plaintive letter from W. J. Davidson, the secretary and general manager at Castlederg:

> I brought your offer for purchase of Coach Body &c. before my Directors at their meeting on 19th instant. I was instructed to write you, that although willing to part with the Coach they think the figure offered is too small. It may be of only scrap value whilst lying here but it will be of very greatly more value to a purchaser to make use of it.
>
> The roller bearings (SKF Co.) which are in perfect order on the

wheels cost more than the £25 offered.

After all I think we are entitled to get something more out of the sale, so that this Company won't lose all and another Company gain all in the transaction.

After some discussion, £25 was accepted. Forbes wrote to Glover of the purchase:

... while admitting the derelict motor coach is of only scrap value to them, the purchaser should pay a fancy price for it because of some inherent or problematical value it may have that apparently they have failed to discover. Of course one must make allowance for the pangs of parenthood in a disappointing offspring.

The railcar was towed to Victoria Bridge on 4 January 1933, and was taken to Strabane over the Great Northern and thence to Stranorlar. It was decided to power the vehicle, and it was given a six-cylinder Reo FA engine. As No. 2, it had a life of 11 years thus, in spite of the comments of H. E. Wilson who wrote from the Dundalk drawing office to G. T. Glover on 13 October 1934:

When at Stranorlar yesterday I inspected this Car and found that, although only a four-wheeled vehicle, it is fitted with a 'Bissell' truck at the front. Theoretically this is, of course, unsound. I did not travel on the vehicle but Mr Forbes informed me that its running is quite satisfactory. The transmission, with the Edwards Worm Drive at the rear and the Hoffmann Boxes with frame etc. at front has been well fitted up and is a satisfactory job. The vehicle is in regular service.

By April 1944 railcar No. 2 had been lying at Glenties for nearly three years, out of use due to cannibalisation of the engine. It was decided to rebuild it yet again, and make it a trailer. This involved lengthening the frame by about 3 ft; the seating was increased from 16 to 30. The conversion allowed Trailer No. 13 to be scrapped, and Trailer No. 2 continued in use until the end of 1959, the epitome of the late Henry Forbes' pursuit of economy.

Railcars No. 14 and No. 15 began work in February 1935 and April 1936 and were generally similar to No. 12. As before, Walker Bros supplied the diesel traction portions, powered by the Gardner 6L2 engines, and the Great Northern works completed the construction. No. 14 had the half-cab of its elders and No. 15 the more fashionable full cab. In both, the windows could be lowered for ventilation, whereas No. 12 had small top lights. They ran for a time, about 1945, with their bodies transposed. In March 1953, No. 14 was given a Gardner 5LW engine. The total mileages credited to Nos. 14 and 15 were respectively 896,044 and 866,001.

Railcars 16, 17 and 18 followed in December 1936, August 1938 and December 1940, and were all Walker—GNR built. Articulated, and with a wheel arrangement like Nos. 12, 14 and 15, they were somewhat heavier and had the Gardner 6LW engine of 102 b.h.p. Seating accommodation was 41 in No. 16 and 43 in the other two. No. 16 had a comparatively uneventful life, surviving to the end and running 862,347 miles in all. No. 17 was wrecked beyond repair, and its driver and two of its passengers killed in the collision near Donegal in August 1949. No. 18 was accidentally burned in November 1949 at Sessiaghoneill, and was rebuilt at Dundalk; it returned to service in June 1950 and ran a total of 641,694 miles.

The closure of the Clogher Valley Railway in 1942 made available a further railcar, which was promptly purchased by the Donegal and became its second No. 10. It had been bought from Walker Bros in 1932, and with the Gardner 6L2 engine it was the first articulated power-bogie railcar to run in Ireland. Transferred to Donegal, it served well until the end, and ran up a total of 348,977 miles. After being used for demolition work, it finally joined the other exhibits in the Belfast Transport Museum.

The exigencies of war and its aftermath prevented any further additions to the railcar fleet for seven years. By 1949 it was clear that some of the older cars were worn out and Nos. 7, 8 and 9 were withdrawn. The destruction of No. 17 caused a definite shortage before new stock could arrive. Then, in January 1950, railcar No. 19 was put into service, of the same general design as the previous six cars, but improved as a result of experience. The driver's cab was full fronted, and it was roomier and extended forward so as completely to enclose the engine, and there were side doors for the driver's use. Walker Bros supplied the power bogie, which had the standard Gardner 6LW engine, transmitting through a Donflex clutch to a four-speed Meadows gearbox and Hardy-Spicer propeller shaft. This had a worm drive to the rear axle of the bogie, whose wheels were linked by side rods. The body, from Dundalk works, seated 41.

A second and similar car, No. 20, joined No. 19 in January 1951. Both ran until the end of 1959, amounting total mileages of 371,096 and 348,951 respectively. They were bought by the Isle of Man Railway as their first railcars.

The railcar and trailer stock was thus a varied lot, much of it having an interesting and chequered history. Among the 23 vehicles, seven were second-hand, their purchase illustrating Forbes's interest in his developing railcar project, their cost and subsequent history showing the ever-present need to economise and to get maximum value from each vehicle.

Light wagons, both open and sheeted and covered, were used behind the railcars. To distinguish them from ordinary goods wagons they were painted red. The tractive power of the railcars was calculated on the 'ordinary wagon basis' and was given in the appendices to the working timetables as follows:

Section	Railcar Numbers							
	Petrol				Diesel			
	1	2/6	3	4/9/10	7/8	10	11	12, 14, 15, 16, 17, 18, 19, 20
Letterkenny	—	1	—	1	2	2	2	2
Finn Valley	1	2	1	2	4	3	5	3 (12 & 14 originally 4)
Glenties	—	1	—	1	2	—	4	—
West Donegal	—⎫							
Ballyshannon	—⎬ 1	—	1		2	2	3	2
Killybegs	—⎭							

It was also stated that on level stretches of these sections where the journey was not continuous, the Finn Valley figures might be applied. For calculation, the average weight of a red wagon or a trailer was taken as three tons empty and four tons loaded, an ordinary wagon was four tons empty and six tons loaded.

Familiarity in the use of the railcars seems to have bred a certain degree of contempt for the potential dangers of jumping down on to the ballast. The 1939 edition of the appendix to the working timetable contained the following significant section:

> Rail Car drivers must prevent employees or ordinary passengers entering or leaving the rail cars when in motion and those who persist in this should be reported. Permanent way men are to be particularly warned of this, they are not as a rule active in their movements.
>
> Drivers must see that the printed notice is pasted up in the cars warning all concerned of this danger so that in the event of an accident the Committee may be protected.

CARRIAGE STOCK

The broad-gauge stock of the Finn Valley Company, seven

coaching and 27 merchandise vehicles, was purchased in April 1874 from Brown, Marshalls & Co. of the Britannia Railway Carriage & Wagon Works, Birmingham. The coaching vehicles consisted of two tricomposite carriages, two thirds, two third-brake vans, one carriage truck and one horse box. The merchandise vehicles were made up of four open and 23 covered wagons. The total stock remained unaltered for 22 years, until sold to the Dublin, Wicklow & Wexford Railway. Four open and 23 closed wagons are listed in the Finn Valley returns for the end of 1890, but as the half-yearly report of the DW & W for the second half of 1894 states that two open and 25 covered wagons had been received from the FVR, two of the open wagons may have been reconstructed in the interim. Nothing is known of the livery of the FVR vehicles.

The narrow-gauge carriage stock is listed in Table 6. The West Donegal began work in 1882 with 11 carriages, all six-wheelers built by the Railway Carriage & Wagon Co. The extreme pairs of wheels had a lateral motion to assist passage on curves. Seven of these West Donegal carriages were converted to covered wagons at Stranorlar at various dates between 1926 and 1930, these additions to the goods stock being necessary in view of customs examination delays. Three others of the six-wheelers were scrapped and one remains: No. 1, a panelled saloon, originally first class, now preserved in the Transport Museum at Belfast. This has end compartments each with two fixed armchairs, a flap table and end windows. Doors led to two inner compartments and the side lavatory. Nos. 2 and 3 began as tricomposites, arranged third, second, first, first, second, and had horizontal oval lights over the side windows of the compartments. The lower half of the bodies were boarded, the upper half panelled. The five thirds (Nos. 4-8) had straight, matchboarded sides, panelled ends and wooden slatted seats. Panelled sides and ends characterised Nos. 9-11, the three second-third brakes in which the three passenger compartments were together. The guards' look-outs were at the extreme end. All the 1882 carriages had curved sides.

The next purchase, of 17 carriages from the Oldbury Carriage & Wagon Co. in 1893, was needed to cope with the Killybegs extension, and the regauging which came the following year on the old FVR section, together with the opening of the line to Glenties in 1895. All were bogie vehicles. Originally five were tricompos (Nos. 12 and 14-17), arranged 2, 2, 1, 1, 3. No. 13 was a first-third compo., unusual in having the thirds seated logitudinally in two end compartments. Both it and the six third brake vans (Nos. 23-28) had straight sides of vertical matchboarding, the rest having curved sides.

Oldbury also supplied six thirds in 1901. These were 5 ft longer than any of the earlier carriages. Nos. 29 and 30 were light vehicles with two compartments, for smokers and non-smokers. Originally they had panelled sides and end verandahs, but at a later date the verandahs were closed in. The roofs sloped towards the ends. No. 30 was given roller bearings and bus-type seats and was latterly used as a railcar trailer on the Letterkenny road. Nos. 31-34 were orthodox, six-compartment vehicles.

In 1905 nine carriages were supplied by Pickering of Wishaw. Four, Nos. 35-38, were lavatory 1st/2nd composites, arranged 1, L, 1, 2, L, 2. The first class end had three rectangular observation windows. Nos. 39 and 40 were officially termed corridor thirds, they were in fact saloons, each had two compartments opening off end verandahs when built. Later, the verandahs were boxed in and entry given by side doors at each end. In their latter state they seated 60, facing towards end observation windows. The last three Pickering vehicles were Nos. 41-43; these had a single 3rd compartment at each end, and a large guard's compartment between them. Side duckets were provided, and double doors opened outwards to give access to a space 23 ft 4½ in. in length.

The Strabane & Letterkenny Railway Company accounted for the 13 carriages which came from Oldbury in 1907. The eight thirds, Nos. 44-51, were similar to Nos. 31-34 of 1900. No. 51 was later converted to a 3, 2, 1, 1, 2, 3, tricompo, akin to Nos. 55, 56 of this era. Nos. 52-54 were second-third brake vans, with two thirds at the ends of the vehicle, and a guard's compartment 19 ft 2½ in. long.

The total of 56 carriages was maintained until 1926, when railcar working started and conversion of the old West Donegal six-wheelers began. By 1930 the total was down to 43, and to 39 and 37 in 1940 and 1950 respectively. During this time the S & L stock remained constant at 13 vehicles, so that the reductions in the total affected only the Joint Committee's stock.

In 1950, the Ulster Transport Authority ended narrow-gauge operations in County Antrim and the coaches which had been used on the Ballycastle line became redundant. Three of them, built by the Northern Counties Committee in the Belfast shops in 1928 for the Ballymena—Larne boat trains, were sold to the Joint Committee at a total purchase price of £1,399. The first to transfer was No. 352, which went to Stranorlar in August 1951 and after painting and overhaul was used as No. 57 of the Joint Committee's stock. Nos.

318(58) and 351(59) followed in January 1951. All three were electrically lighted, in contrast to the acetylene of the existing Donegal stock.

Nos. 57 and 59 were much the longest carriages to run on the Donegal system, being 50 ft over headstocks and 52 ft 4 in. over buffers. Across the roof they measured 7 ft 10½ in., while all the other Donegal carriages were but 7 ft 4 in. On the Ballymena—Larne road they had used end corridor connections, but by the time they reached Donegal these had been blanked off. The body of No. 58 was also of corridor type, but was built on an 1879 underframe. Its lengths over headstocks and over buffers were 41 ft 3½ in. and 43 ft 7½ in., with the same roof width as Nos. 57-59. On all these NCC carriages the buffer centres were 2 ft from rail level, and for Donegal trains the buffers had to be raised by 10½ in.

There appear to have been five identifiable carriage liveries. The earliest has been described as Indian red or chocolate, lined in peacock blue, with the class numbers and names in gold, shaded black and red. Two photographs at Stranorlar show Nos. 29 and 37 apparently in this livery, and are interesting in that the classes are identified only by a large number on the door; these photographs show light-coloured horizontal lines at the waist and step level, doubtless the peacock-blue lining referred to above.

Probably during the currency of the red livery, R. H. Livesey had the saloon carriage specially painted in a two colour scheme : black on the lower half and dark cream above. Livesey also introduced a general two-colour livery of plum and cream, with the mouldings in signal red. The 1905 batch of Pickering carriages is seen from maker's photographs to have borne this livery, and with white roofs, footboards and wheel rims, they must have been exceptionally smart in appearance. Classes were marked on the doors at waist level as 'FIRST' etc., and the two saloons, Nos. 39 and 40 had 'THIRD CLASS' in full below the waist line on each compartment.

During Livesey's time, the livery was again altered, the two-colour effect being replaced by black. The lining of this sombre livery has been stated by R. W. A. Salter to be red, but Stranorlar personnel appear to agree that it was in fact white.

Finally, during the 1930s, a two-colour livery was again introduced with red lower and cream upper part, separated by a thin black line. The ends of the coaches were entirely red, except for those with end observation windows where the two colours were carried round. The underframes, buffer beams and bogies and roofs were black. End steps and acetylene generators were either red or black. Numbers were in gold, shaded black, and were carried either between the waist mouldings or between the windows.

The crest of the Donegal Railway Co., and later of the Joint Committee, was either below the waist line, or on a circular board at mid-window level, just above the number.

WAGON STOCK

The original West Donegal stock of 40 covered wagons, three open wagons and two brake vans would have taken the series up to No. 45, but the brake vans would appear to have been renumbered at some stage and are probably represented by Nos. 209 and 210, the latter eventually becoming a breakdown van for a time. Some of the West Donegal stock appears to have been rebuilt into combined goods, horse and cattle trucks.

By the end of 1895, the Donegal Railway stock comprised 95 covered and cattle wagons, 23 open wagons, 17 ballast wagons and two brake vans. This was maintained to the turn of the century, though by then the total available stock had actually increased under the Killybegs and Glenties Parliamentary Orders of 1890 and 1891. To the lines built under these Orders were allocated 38 and 40 wagons respectively, ten in each case being flats.

By the last year of the Donegal Railway Company's existence the stock numbered 135 covered, 75 open and 23 ballast wagons. Since much of the merchandise went in mixed trains, only two brake vans were needed.

Under the Joint Committee the stock continued to grow, much of it coming in as Strabane & Letterkenny-owned wagons. The 'Separate Undertaking' to Derry was credited with owning 39 open wagons. By 1912 the total of goods and service vehicles was 312, made up of 145 covered, 89 open and tranship wagons, eight combined carriage, timber and coal trucks (according to the half-yearly report), 18 ballast wagons and two brake vans. In addition the s & l had 40 covered and ten open wagons.

In 1927 the conversion of old carriages into covered vans was begun, three or four vehicles per year being altered. The resulting commodious vans were of great assistance to customs examination, which by then had been in vogue for four years, since good-capacity wagons capable of being sealed were in demand. Both six-wheeled and bogie wagons thus joined an almost exclusively four-wheeled wagon stock. Some of the ex-carriages were later reconverted to flat wagons.

Even after Forbes's death, the Stranorlar genius for improvisation led to the use of old boiler tubes for the sides of peat-carrying wagons. Three such vehicles were made, Nos. 315, 321 and 323; No. 315 was also used to carry new motor cars and scrap metal.

Wagon livery was grey, though for a time some had to suffer the hygienic indignity of being tarred, since Forbes felt that this was cheaper than paint. Lettering was in white. In the Minute Book it is recorded on 22 October 1906 that rolling stock was to be lettered 'D.R.C.'. Later 'C.D.R.' was in use, then under Forbes a monogram of 'D' and 'R' overlapping, and finally 'DR'.

Numbered at 1-23, separately from both the carriage and the goods wagons, were the 'red wagons', as they were both colloquially and officially termed—the light wagons designed to be towed by the railcars. Earlier numbers were open wagons, ex the Castlederg & Victoria Bridge Tramway, with an inverted V top or a bar for a sheet cover. Later additions were covered and came from the Clogher Valley line. They were rebuilt at Stranorlar, but initially gave rise to endless minor derailments and only after repeated visits to the shops did they settle down. Numbered in the red-wagon series was a small breakdown van (No. 1), whose genesis had been a flat wagon, but which in its final state sported a corrugated iron roof and open sides. The red wagons were painted the same colour as the engines and railcars, with black roofs and white lettering.

Since contact was made with the L & LS at Letterkenny and at Derry there was some interchange of wagon stock between the two lines. This was, however, not entirely simple since the L & LS wagons had different vacuum-brake pipes, buffer heights and coupling hooks. So that the different brake bags could be linked together, reducing couplers were used. At one time unbraked L & LS wagons could be included in Donegal trains if marshalled at the rear of the train.

The buffer height of the Swilly wagons, 2 ft 7½ in., was 3 in. less than that of the Donegal's wagons. With interchange in mind, all the Hurst Nelson wagons bought in 1908-9, 40 of them covered and ten open, were fitted with a special type of two-storey buffer which had a long head and two coupling pins.

Vacuum brakes were fitted to all the Company's vehicles.

Since writing the above, two valuable and detailed papers on the history of the carriage and wagon stock have been written by Mr S. J. Carse and have been published in the Journal of the Irish Railway Record Society. They are listed under 'Sources' on page 201.

CHAPTER VIII

Conclusion

RAILS SERVE A VANISHING POPULATION

How many thousands of Donegal folk made their last journey on Irish soil by train down the Finn valley will never be known exactly. With an emigrant's ticket in their pocket, and the Atlantic liner waiting in Lough Foyle, the new world across the ocean seemed to offer more to many of them than life among the hills of Donegal.

It was into such an environment that the Finn Valley Railway was launched, 15 years after the disastrous Famine. The 4th Viscount Lifford and his friends put much of their energies and fortunes into the scheme, which they hoped would bring prosperity to their county. Their enthusiasm was to be damped by rising costs even before the line was completed. In spite of continuing depopulation, and a hinterland that was picturesque rather than prosperous, the Finn Valley and its narrow-gauge follower, the West Donegal, eventually succeeded in forging a rail link through the Barnesmore Gap as far west as the county town.

During the 1880s and '90s, a benevolent British Government, having decided upon a solution to the problem of poverty in Ireland, was building railways in the remoter parts and arranging for them to be worked by existing companies. So the Killybegs and the Glenties lines came to be added to the 32 miles of privately-built railway and they brought with them a measure of prosperity. The Donegal Railway Company, successor to the FVR and the WDR from 1892, then built branches to Ballyshannon and to Derry, and another company connected Strabane with Letterkenny.

Of commuter traffic there was practically none and the income had to depend largely on the movement of goods, principally agricultural produce and imported coal. Summer tourists and livestock traffic from the periodic cattle fairs together made their contribution, but were insufficient to give a balanced long-term economy. By 1906, the Donegal Railway Company was glad enough

Seals of the constituents

to sell its assets to the Midland Railway of England and the Great Northern of Ireland, who combined to run it by a Joint Committee.

Four years after the formation of the County Donegal Railways Joint Committee in 1906, Henry Forbes came from the Great Northern of Ireland to succeed W. R. Lawson as secretary and accountant and in time he became manager.

Forbes's energetic and forceful personality soon became felt at Stranorlar, and he had to deal with the vicissitudes of railway operation during World War I and then in a country troubled by civil disorders. In the early 1920s Ireland became divided politically : the CDRJC acquired an international character, since the major part, in County Donegal, was in the Irish Free State, while Strabane, a few miles of the old Finn Valley line and the branch to Derry were in Northern Ireland.

No sooner were these hurdles negotiated than car and lorry traffic on the roads began for the first time to challenge the supremacy of the railway. To keep his railway alive, Forbes instituted a vigorous policy of economy, and from 1926 the comparatively light passenger services began to be worked by railcars. Indeed it may be truly said that the Donegal cradled much of Britain's railcar development, a process made possible by the co-operation of the mechanical engineering staff of the Great Northern. The Donegal's management had the wisdom to integrate the local road bus service with their trains, and for many years the combination withstood the impact of road transport and provided a thinly-populated area with a very satisfactory transport service.

The drastic economies of the 1930s, followed as they were by material shortages during World War II, brought the Donegal Railways to a premature end. Deferred permanent-way maintenance had resulted in the imposition of speed restrictions and a stage was eventually reached when complete relaying of much of the track had become a necessity. The two owners were by this time themselves in financial straits. The necessary capital was not forthcoming to perpetuate a service that was unlikely to bring profits. Throughout 1959 the railway functioned as vigorously as ever and then, greatly to the regret of the countryside which it served, it ceased operating at the end of the year. As its northern neighbour, the Londonderry & Lough Swilly Railway, had already done, the CDRJC then perforce turned to moving freight and passengers on the roads.

Appendices

1 : LIST OF STATIONS AND HALTS

FINN VALLEY SECTION

(Opened 7 September 1863. Closed to passengers 1 January 1960, to goods 25 January 1960)

	Miles	Class-ification	Crane Power (tons)	Remarks
Stranorlar	0	GPFLHC	3	
Town Bridge	½		-	Halt, closed about 1950
Cavan	1¾		-	Halt
Killygordon	4	LHC	-	
Liscooly	5¾	GP	-	
Castlefinn	7¾	LHC	-	
Clady	9¾	LHC	-	Halt
Strabane	13¾	FLHC	5	

WEST DONEGAL SECTION

(Opened to Druminin 25 April 1882. Opened to Donegal 16 September 1889. Closed 1 January 1960)

	Miles	Class-ification	Crane Power (tons)	Remarks
Stranorlar	0	GPFLHC	3	
Meenglas	2½	P*	-	Halt
Derg Bridge	8		-	Halt, opened 2 Decr. 1912
Barnesmore	12	P*	-	Formerly Barrack Bridge Halt
Lough Eske	14	PL	-	Named Druminin until 1889
Clar Bridge	16	P	-	
Donegal	18	GPFLHC	3	

Page 183: LONDONDERRY VICTORIA ROAD STATION

(above) Locomotive No. 1 'Alice' (Class 5a) on afternoon Derry-Strabane train, 22 August 1950; (below) Locomotive No. 6 'Columbkille' and Strabane train, 24 August 1951. The two-deck bridge over the River Foyle is visible beyond the platform

Page 184: BY THE LINESIDE

(above) Locomotive No. 8 'Foyle' (Class 2) on mixed train between Fintown and Glenties, July 1924; (below) Group at Castlefinn, 1 January 1960

KILLYBEGS SECTION.
(Opened 18 August 1893. Closed 1 January 1960)

	Miles	Class-ification	Crane Power (tons)	Remarks
Donegal	0	GPFLHC	3	
Killymard	2	P*	-	Halt, closed 1956
Mountcharles	4	GPFL	5	
Doorin Road	5¾	P	-	Made a halt in 1921
Mullanboy	7¼		-	Halt
Inver	8¼	GPLHC	-	
Port	10	P	-	Made a halt in 1913
Dunkineely	12¼	GPLHC	1½	
Spamount	13¼		-	Opened about 1944
Bruckless	14½	GP	-	Made a halt in 1924
Ardara Road	16¾	GP	-	Made a halt in 1910
Killybegs	19	GPFLHC	-	

GLENTIES SECTION
(Opened 3 June 1895. Closed except for occasional turf, livestock and bog iron ore trains, 13 December 1947. Closed completely 12 March 1952)

	Miles	Class-ification	Crane Power (tons)	Remarks
Stranorlar	0	GPFLHC	3	
Ballybofey	½	GP	-	
Glenmore	4	GP	-	
Cloghan	6¾		-	
Elaghtagh	9		-	Halt, opened July 1930
Glassagh	11½		-	Halt, opened March 1937
Ballinamore	13¾	GP	-	
Fintown	16	GPLHC	-	
Shallogans	21	P*	-	
Glenties	24	GPLHC	1½	

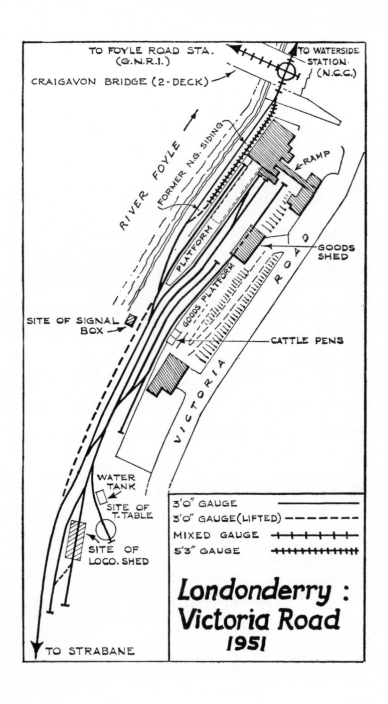

TO FOYLE ROAD STA.
(G.N.R.I.)

TO WATERSIDE
STATION·
(N.C.C.)

CRAIGAVON BRIDGE (2-DECK)

RIVER FOYLE

FORMER N.G. SIDING

RAMP

GOODS
SHED

PLATFORM

GOODS PLATFORM

SITE OF SIGNAL
BOX

CATTLE PENS

VICTORIA   ROAD

WATER
TANK

SITE OF
T. TABLE

3'0" GAUGE ──────────

3'0" GAUGE(LIFTED) ──────────

MIXED GAUGE +++++++

5'3" GAUGE ++++++++++++

SITE OF
LOCO. SHED

TO STRABANE

Londonderry :
Victoria Road
1951

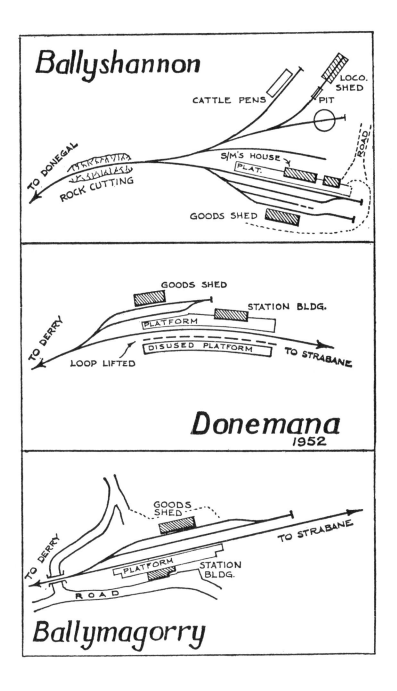

LONDONDERRY SECTION

(Opened for goods 1 August 1900, for passengers 6 August 1900.
Closed 1 January 1955)

	Miles	Class-ification	Crane Power (tons)	Remarks
Strabane	0	GPFLHC	5	
Ballymagorry	2¾	GPL	-	
Ballyheather	4½	P*	-	Halt
Donemana	6¼	GPLH	-	
Cullion	8¼	GPLH	-	
Desertone	9½	P	-	Halt
Newbuildings	11¾	P	-	
Londonderry (Victoria Road)	14½	GPLH	5	

BALLYSHANNON SECTION

(Opened 2 September 1905. Closed 1 January 1960)

	Miles	Class-ification	Crane Power (tons)	Remarks
Donegal	0	GPFLHC	3	
Hospital	½		-	Halt
Drumbar	1½	P*	-	Halt
Laghey	3¼	GPLHC	-	Halt latterly
Bridgetown	5	GPLHC	-	Halt latterly
Ballintra	7	GPLHC	-	
Dromore	8		-	Halt
Dorrian's Bridge	9		-	Halt
Rossnowlagh	10¼	GPLHC	-	Made a halt in 1924
Friary Halt	10½		-	Opened 1 March 1953
Coolmore	11		-	Halt, opened 1929
Creevy	12¾	P*	-	Halt, opened 1911
Ballyshannon	15½	GPLHC	-	

STRABANE & LETTERKENNY RAILWAY

	Miles	Class-ification	Crane Power (tons)	Remarks
Strabane	0	GPFLHC	5	
Lifford	1	P*	-	Halt
Ballindrait	2¾	GP	-	
Coolaghy	4¾	P*	¾	Halt
Raphoe	6½	GPFLHC	-	
Convoy	9	GPFLHC	-	
Cornagillagh	11	P*	-	Halt, opened 1911
Glenmaquin	13¾	GPL	-	
Letterkenny	19¼	GPFLHC	-	

NOTE: Classification and Crane Power (where given) is abstracted from *Official Handbook of Railway Stations*, published in 1911 by the Railway Clearing House. Abbreviations used are: G=Goods. P=Passengers and parcels. P*=Passengers, but not parcels or miscellaneous traffic. F=Furniture vans, Carriages, Portable engines and Machines on wheels. L=Live stock. H= Horse boxes and prize cattle vans. C=Carriages by passenger train.

In the 1956 edition of the *Handbook*, Cavan, Derg Bridge, Mullanboy, Coolmore and Dromore are all classified P*. Spamount, Cloghan, Elaghtagh and Glassagh are not listed. Laghey, Bridgetown, Glenmaquin and Rossnow-lagh are reduced to P*.

2 : LOCOMOTIVE DRIVERS, FIREMEN AND RAILCAR DRIVERS IN THE SERVICE OF THE CDRJC AT THE END OF 1959

	Years of service
Locomotive drivers	
William J. McMenamin	39
Patrick Gallagher	14
Locomotive firemen	
Francis McMenamin	48
William McFeely	47
James McKenna	45
Tractor driver	
Joseph Foy	41
Railcar drivers	
Martin Herron	36
Joseph Thompson	29
Patrick Hannigan	18
Cathal Kennedy	15
Collins Laverty	14
John McCallion	14
Christie Kennedy	12
Michael Gallen	10

3 : PUBLIC ROAD LEVEL CROSSING GATES

* signifies connected with Up Distant Signal
† signifies connected with Down Distant Signal
x signifies telephone or bell communication

STRABANE—KILLYBEGS

1	*	*Liscooly station* (Schoales)
2	x	*Lough Eske station*
3		McNamee
4	*	McClanaghy
5		McHugh
6		Gorrell
7		*Donegal station gates*
8		McDaid
9		McGroarty
10	†	Bogle
11	*	Keeney
12	†	Meehan
13	†	Freeburn
14		*Doorin Road station*
15	†	Keeney
16	†	*Mullanboy* (Rose)
17	†	Scott
18		Conaghan (railcar stop)
19	*	Cannon
20		Battles (railcar stop)
21		Meehan
22		Rose (railcar stop)
23		*Dunkineely station*
24	†	Lappin
25		McMenamin
26		Kenny, later McGroarty
26A		*Bruckless station*
27		McMenamin
28		*Ardara Road station* (Gillespie)
29		McGinley, later Boyle
30	*	Hegarty (railcar stop)

STRANORLAR—GLENTIES

31		*Ballybofey station*
32	*	McConnell
33		McBride
34		*Glenmore station*
35		*Ballinamore station* (Doherty)
36	*	Doherty (railcar stop)
37		Herron
38	*	McMonagle (railcar stop)
39		McNelis
40		**Glenties station**

DONEGAL—BALLYSHANNON

41	McHugh (railcar stop)
42 †	Monaghan
43 †	Conaghan
44	*Bridgetown station* (Gallagher)
45	McAree
46 *	*Creevy Halt* (McIntyre)
47	Culleton

STRABANE—LETTERKENNY

48	O'Brien
49	Devenny
50 †	Donnelly
51	Kearns
52 †	Chembers
53	Linney (railcar stop)
54 †	Mulrine
55 * x	Gillen
56 x	Kelly, later Cannon, later Vance (railcar stop)
57	Doherty
58	Parke
59 *	Maguire
60 *	Martin
61 †	Gillen
62 *	Baird

Notes. There were three crossing gates on the Strabane—Londonderry section.

In the above table, gates at Stations or Halts and under the direct control of the station staff, are printed in italics, and the name given is that of the station or halt. In general the other gates, some of which were scheduled railcar stopping places, were known by the name of the family or person occupying the gate house. The number was seldom used, and passengers asked for tickets to 'Battle's' or 'Conaghan's', sometimes to the surprise of the visitor with his timetable and map. The crossings and the crossing keepers' kitchens were traditionally part of the railway.

4 : NOTES ON TICKETS

By C. R. GORDON STUART*

The earliest tickets of the Donegal group were those of the Finn Valley Railway. Originally, first-class *singles* were white, second-class *singles* blue and third-class buff. *Returns* of these three classes were all one colour, namely yellow, pink and green respectively. Later, towards the end of the 1880s, the colours of the returns were altered to yellow and white, blue and pink, and blue and green respectively for the three classes. *Excursions* were white with one, two or three horizontal red lines through the ticket to denote the class.

The next section of the group to open was the West Donegal Railway. Tickets on the line followed the general later colour scheme of the Finn Valley, namely white, blue and buff for first-, second- and third-class *singles*, the *returns* being yellow and white, pink and blue and green and buff respectively. *Excursions* were also white, and had the same colour scheme of red bands as had those of the FVR. The *dog* tickets, yellow and red in colour, are good examples of the 'non-passenger' tickets used by most of the smaller Irish railways round about the 1890s.

The year 1892 witnessed the amalgamation of the FVR and the WDR into the Donegal Railway, and from that date the tickets were headed Donegal Railway. The basic colours for the tickets remained unaltered, carrying on the same colour scheme and design of printing as the WDR, so there is no need to repeat the details. However several special classes of traffic began to develop and special rates came into being which had not been in force when the old Companies were in existence and thus any collection of Donegal Railway tickets became a galaxy of colour. Special tickets were printed for people who travelled on *harvesting*, their colour being buff with a red horizontal band through the centre. Other interesting tickets were those for both emigrants and immigrants; these were green and were sold at amazingly cheap rates, an emigrant's *single* from Killybegs to Londonderry only costing 3s. 8d. *Week-end* tickets were put into use, in addition to *excursion* tickets and these followed the usual colour schemes according to class, but had a white circle on either half, while *market returns* followed the usual class colour arrangements, but had the one, two or three horizontal red bands overprinted, similar to the *excursion* tickets, which however remained white for all three classes. The *dog* tickets changed to white with three yellow horizontal bands, and the *bicycle* tickets were brick-red with a glazed surface. There also exists an interesting series of paper blank tickets for local journeys, issued from places where there was no booking office open; these seemed to vary in colour according to the station of issue. Barnesmore was yellow, Clar Bridge pink, Killymard blue, Meenglas green, and Ballyheather was a colour which is best described as flesh.

From 1 May 1906, the Donegal Railways became the joint property of the GNR and the NCC, and tickets were thenceforward headed CDRJC, excepting

---

* This Appendix is reproduced with minor alterations from H. Fayle's book *Narrow Gauge Railways of Ireland*, in which it was an Appendix. The author is indebted to the late Mr Fayle, and to Mr C. R. Gordon Stuart for permission.

those tickets issued on the section between Londonderry and Strabane, which, being entirely NCC property issued tickets headed NCCMR. The new Joint Committee tickets followed fully upon the colour schemes of the old Donegal Railway. More modern times brought new issues, and as the railway had an arrangement with some local bus undertakings in their area for pooling traffic, special tickets were issued in exchange for the *return* portions of bus tickets and these were coloured yellow and red. More *excursion* issues of a special nature emanated, such as *weekly* and *day trip* tickets, whilst the *dog* tickets lost one of their yellow stripes and the *bicycle* tickets became a more drab red and were no longer glazed. Towards the end of the 1930s, the CDRJC, which had already abolished second class on 1 January 1922, seeing that the majority of its traffic was being worked by diesel cars of one class only, decided to abolish first class also and henceforth tickets were issued in the old third class colours, but with no mention of the class printed on them. Also, for a very short while before then, all tickets issued at stations located in Eire, which actually means all stations excepting Strabane, had their tickets printed by an Eire firm to avoid payment of customs duty and these tickets were actually printed at the Dublin works of the GSR. Present-day tickets of the CDRJC are of rather sad appearance, some of the mid-1940s being on totally uncoloured strawboard in the case of the *singles* and *returns*, while the *bicycle* tickets are just plain white.

On 1 January 1909 the Strabane and Letterkenny Railway started operations and issued tickets of its own headed STRABANE & LETTERKENNY RLY. CO.; this was later printed as S. & L. Ry. Co. There is no need to go further into their story, for the colour scheme followed that of the CDRJC very closely. Only a few of them ever reached the stage of being printed by the GSR at Dublin, though the writer has a couple of such printings, but at about that time it was decided to head the tickets to conform with the remainder of the Donegal system, that is CDRJC. Prior to the printing of the Eire station tickets by the Dublin works of the GSR, tickets of the Donegal and the Strabane & Letterkenny Railways were printed by the same printers who produced tickets for the GNR, and a very strong resemblance can be traced between them at all periods from 1906 onwards.

Before leaving the Donegal group, it is worth noting that this was the only Irish narrow-gauge railway to issue a *weekly run-about* ticket at 10s, available over the entire system, excepting the Strabane—Londonderry section. Also, a *bicycle season* at a special rate was available if required.

Finn Valley Railway Company

Chairmen—

1860-88	Viscount Lifford
1888-92	Sir Samuel H. Hayes, Bart.

Secretaries—

1860	Sir Edwin Hayes, Bart.
1860-61	— Murphy
1861-90	James Alex. Ledlie
1890-92	R. H. Livesey

Engineers—

1860-69	John Bower
1869-71	John Stokes
1872	R. T. Hutton
1872-88	Robert Collins
1888-91	Abraham McC. Stewart (pro tem)
1891-92	Edward Radcliff

Superintendents of carrying stock—

1878-82	James Larrissy
1882	J. W. Barber

Locomotive superintendents—

1882-90	D. Laverty
1890-92	R. H. Livesey

Accountants—

1861-90	James Alex. Ledlie
1890-92	R. H. Livesey

West Donegal Railway Company

Chairmen—

1879-88	Viscount Lifford
1888-92	William Sinclair

Secretaries—

1879-90	James Alex. Ledlie
1890-92	R. H. Livesey

Donegal Railway Company

Chairmen—

1892-96	William Sinclair
1896-1904	Sir James Musgrave
1904-1906	John A. Pomeroy

General manager—

1897-1906	R. H. Livesey

Secretaries and accountants—

1892-1897	R. H. Livesey
1897-1906	W. R. Lawson

Engineers—

1892-97	E. Radcliff
1897-1906	A. McC. Stewart

Locomotive superintendent—

1892-1906	R. H. Livesey

Co. Donegal Railways Joint Committee

Secretaries—

1906-10	W. R. Lawson
1910-43	Henry Forbes (Secretary and Traffic Manager 1916-28, thereafter Secretary and Manager)
1943-66	Bernard L. Curran (Secretary and Manager)
1966-	E. Fitzgerald (Manager)
1966-	M. J. Hayes (Secretary)

Accountants—

1906-07	W. R. Lawson
1907-17	John Shields (Book-keeper) Accountant 1917-25
1925-38	Peter Whitelaw
1938-43	Bernard L. Curran
1943-65	W. J. Purvis
1965-	R. G. Watt

Locomotive superintendents—

1906-07	R. H. Livesey
1907-22	R. M. Livesey

Locomotive engineers—

1922-33	George T. Glover
1933-39	George B. Howden
1939-50	H. McIntosh
1950-57	R. W. Meredith
1957-60	H. E. Wilson

Engineers—

1906-07	R. H. Livesey
1907-22	R. M. Livesey
1922-31	W. K. Wallace
1931-33	H. P. Stewart
1933-35	R. L. McIlmoyle
1935-56	Neil C. Cain
1956-60	W. A. Hill

Strabane, Raphoe & Convoy Railway and Strabane & Letterkenny Railway Companies

Chairmen—

1903-1911	T. B. Stoney
1911-1921	P. McMenamin
1921-22	Edward McFadden
1922-60	J. C. Herdman

Secretaries and accountants—

1903-10	W. R. Lawson
1910-1943	Henry Forbes
1943-1960	Bernard L. Curran

Engineers and locomotive superintendents—

As for C.D.R.J.C. until 1922

Locomotive engineers—

As for C.D.R.J.C. from 1922

Engineers—

As for C.D.R.J.C. from 1922

6 : WAGON STOCK

Numbers	Maker	Date	Tare	To carry	Remarks
1-40	Oldbury	1881	3.12.0	6.0.0	covered (WDR)
41-43	,,	1881			flat (WDR), 42 conv. to tranship
44	,,	1893			open tranship
45	,,	1900			flat
46-95	,,	1893	4.7.0	6.0.0	covered
96-100	,,	1893	4.5.0	6.0.0	cattle
101-120	,,	1893			flat
121-154	,,	1900	4.0.0	6.0.0	flat
155	,,	1900			tranship, covered
156/7	,,	1900			flat
158	Met. C & W	1905	4.0.0	6.0.0	flat
159	Oldbury	1900	7.18.3	14.0.0	bogie flat
160/8	Met. C & W	1905	4.0.0	6.0.0	flat, low sided
169-198	,,	1905	4.7.0	7.0.0	covered
199-208	Pickering	1905	4.10.0	7.0.0	cattle, later covered
209	Oldbury	1881			wood frame, covered
210	,,	1881			as 209, conv. to breakdown van 1893
211-227	Pauling	1904	3.4.0	6.0.0	flats and ballast
228	Pickering	1912			ex-C & VBT, flat
229-238	,,	1907	4.3.2	7.0.0	S & LR, flats, falling sides
239-248	,,	1907	4.10.2	7.0.0	S & LR, combined goods, horse and cattle
249-254	GNRI	1908	1.14.0	3.0.0	flats, tranship, conv. to covered & coal 1922-31, except No. 251
255-284	H.N.	1908	4.11.1	7.0.0	S & LR, covered
285-294	H.N.	1909	4.14.3	7.0.0	CDR, combined goods, horse and cattle
295-304	H.N.	1909	4.7.3	7.0.0	flats
305	Oldbury	1881			flat, ex-WDR carriage truck
306	,,	1881			flat, ex-WDR carriage truck
307/8	,,	1893			flat, ex-timber truck
309-312	Pickering	1905			flats, ex-timber trucks
313	,,	1905			ex-horse box, conv. to wagon 326 in 1927
314	Oldbury	1893			h/box? conv. to 327
315	,,	1893			h/box? conv. to 329
313[2]	CDRJC	1927	7.15.0	12.0.0	6-wh. flat, underframe from No. 10 carriage
314[2]	CDRJC	1927	7.4.0	14.0.0	6-wh. covered, ex-carr. No. 8
315[2]	CDRJC	1927	7.4.0	14.0.0	6-wh. covered, ex-carr. No. 11
316	CDRJC	1928	9.2.2	12.0.0	bogie covered, ex-carr. No. 19
317	CDRJC	1928	9.2.2	12.0.0	,, ,, ,, No. 18
318	CDRJC	1928	9.2.2	12.0.0	,, ,, ,, No. 22
319	CDRJC	1929	9.2.2	12.0.0	,, ,, ,, No. 20

Numbers	Maker	Date	Tare	To carry	Remarks
320	CDRJC	1929	9.2.2	12.0.0	bogie covered, ex-carr. No. 21
321	CDRJC	1929	7.4.0	14.0.0	6-wh. covered, ex-carr. No. 4
322	CDRJC	1929	10.2.2	12.0.0	bogie covered, ex-carr. No. 29
323	CDRJC	1930	7.4.0	12.0.0	6-wh. covered, ex-carr. No. 7
324	CDRJC	1930	7.4.0	12.0.0	„ „ „ No. 5
325	CDRJC	1930	7.4.0	14.0.0	„ „ „ No. 6
326	CDRJC	1927	4.8.0	7.0.0	covered, ex-horse box 313
327	CDRJC	1927		7.0.0	„ „ „ 314
328	Oldbury			15.0.0	bogie flat, wood frame, ex-C & VBT in 1935
329	Pickering			15.0.0	bogie flat, steel frame, ex-C & VBT in 1935
330	CDRJC	1937	10.2.2	12.0.0	bogie covered, ex-carr. No. 25
331	CDRJC	1937	10.2.2	12.0.0	„ „ „ No. 24
332	CDRJC	1937	10.2.2	12.0.0	„ „ „ No. 27
333	CDRJC	1939	10.2.2	12.0.0	„ „ „ No. 26
334				12.0.0	bogie flat, ex-CVR in 1941
335				5.0.0	4-wh. flat, ex-CVR in 1941, used for oil conveyance
336					bogie low-loader made from carriage frame ex-NCC, and probably originally Ballymena, Cushendall & Red Bay Rly. Used for oil storage in loco. shops
337-342					scrapped covered wagon bodies put on wagons 314^2, 322 and 324 (2 to each wagon)
337^2-340^2					tank wagons purchased from Irish Shell Ltd.
341^2-342^2 343-345					tank wagons purchased from L & LSR

Red Wagon Series

1	Breakdown Van
2	Covered, ex-Clogher Valley Railway
3-9	Flat, exCastlederg & Victoria Bridge Tramway
10-23	Covered, ex-Clogher Valley Railway

Acknowledgements and Sources

In the construction of this book I have benefited from the enthusiasm and practical assistance of many members of the staff of the CDRJC. My thanks are especially due to the former manager, Mr Bernard L. Curran, who was kindness itself during my visits, allowing me to consult documents and devoting much time and trouble in answering my many questions. There must be mentioned his successor, Mr E. Fitzgerald and, in addition, Messrs J. Browne, R. P. Dunnion, P. McBride and R. Parks and the late Mr W. A. Purvis, for without their help much detail would have been overlooked. The companionship of engine and railcar crews on journeys will long be remembered.

Of the former staff of the Great Northern Railway, I was fortunate to have had the stimulus of discussion with the late Mr George B. Howden, and with Mr H. E. Wilson. The reminiscences of their personal involvement in early railcar development were of the greatest interest and value.

Sir Basil McFarland, Bt, kindly allowed me to consult documents formerly in the possession of his father, the late Sir John McFarland. These have yielded interesting information on the building of the Glenties line, as well as data on the growth of railway transport in County Donegal.

Thanks are due to the staffs of the British Railways Historical Records Offices in London and in Edinburgh, who gave me unstinted help in literature searches.

The following have also assisted me in a variety of ways: Messrs S. J. Carse, R. N. Clements, D. G. Coakham, D. J. Dickson, the late H. Fayle, G. R. Mahon, C. R. Gordon Stuart and D. L. Smith.

Price, A. (1896) The location, construction and equipment of light or secondary railways in Ireland. *Trans. Inst. Civil Eng. Ireland*, **25**, 93.

Walker, J. F. (1900) The Donegal Railway. *Railway Mag.*, **6**, 240.

(1906) General Manager as engine driver. *Railway Mag.*, **18**, 171.

Shrubsole, E. (1908) *Picturesque Donegal* (G.N.R.I. Tourist Guide).

Sekon, G. A. (1909) The Strabane & Letterkenny Railway. *Railway Mag.*, **24**, 360.

Livesey, R. M. (1912) Rolling stock on the principal Irish narrow-gauge railways. *Proc. Inst. Mech. Eng.*, *559*.

(1912) The County Donegal Railways Joint Committee. *Railway Mag.*, **31**, 129.

(1913) County Donegal Railways Joint Committee—Level Crossing Gates. *Railway News*, **99**, 140.

Cmd. 10 (1922) *Report of the Railway Commission in Northern Ireland*. H.M.S.O., Belfast.

(1922) *Irish Railways*, **5**. *Report of Commission appointed by Provisional Government*. Dail Eireann Papers, S.O. Dublin.

(1923) An Irish Rail Motor Car. *Railway Mag.*, **53**, 259.

Craven, W. H. (1927) The Derwent Valley Light Railway. *Railway Mag.*, **61**, 105.

Salter, R. W. A. (1931) The County Donegal Railways. *Railway Mag.*, **68**, 125.

(1931) Petrol Railcar on Donegal Railways. *Railway Gaz.*, **54**, 356.

(1931) Diesel Rail Car, Donegal Railways. *Railway Gaz.*, **55**, 437.

(1933) Diesel Traction in Ireland. *Railway Gaz.*, **59**, 836.

(1934) Converted petrol railcar, County Donegal Railways. *Railway Gaz.*, **60**, 401.

(1934) 74 h.p. Diesel Locomotive, C.D.R. *The Locomotive*, **40**, 257.

Fayle, H. (1945) *Narrow Gauge Railways of Ireland*.

Hogan, T. L. & Neylon, T. J. (1950) *Report of Investigation of accident on railway system of C.D.R.J.C., near Donegal, 29 August 1949*. S.O. Dublin.

Carse, S. J. (1952) The County Donegal Railways. *Journ. Irish Railway Record Soc.*, **3**, 5.

Celkin. C. A. (1952) History of Public Transport in Donegal. *Donegal Annual*, **2**, No. 2, 406.

McNeill, D. B. (1956) Ulster Tramways and Light Railways. *Transport Handbook No. 1*, Museum & Art Gallery, Belfast.

Boyd, J. I. C. (1956) Donegal Revisited. *Railway World*, **17**, 315.

Smith, W. A. C. (1957) The County Donegal Railways. *Railway Mag.*, **103**, 297.

(1957) *Report of the Committee of Inquiry into Internal Transport*. S.O. Dublin.

Whitehouse, P. B. (1957) Donegal Excursion in *Narrow Gauge Album*.

Thomson, G. R. (1960) The last days of the County Donegal. *Trains Illus. Summer Annual* (p. 41).

Newcombe, N. W. (1960) The End of the Donegal Railway. *Railway World*, **21**, 166.

Curran, B. L. (1960) Steam and Diesel in Donegal. *Railway Roundabout* (p. 60).

McNeill, D. B. (1960) Coastal Passenger Steamers and Inland Navigations

in the north of Ireland. *Transport Handbook No. 3*, Museum & Art Gallery, Belfast.
Fry, C. L. (1961) County Donegal Railbus. *Model Railway Constructor*, **28,** 163.
Patterson, E. M. (1961) The narrow gauge in Ireland—its growth and decay. *Railway Mag.*, **107,** 75 & 169.
Patterson, E. M. (1962) The Ford Railbuses of the DVLR and where they went. *Railway World*, **23,** 17-18.
Patterson, E. M. (1962) The Donegal derailments. *Railway World*, **23,** 222-226.
Patterson, E. M. (1964) *The Lough Swilly Railway*
Patterson, E. M. (1968) *The Ballymena Lines*
Patterson, E. M. (1972) *The Clogher Valley Railway*
Carse, S. J. (1976) Co. Donegal Railway Wagons 1906-59. *Journ. Irish Railway Record Soc.*, **12,** 234.
Carse, S. J. (1980) CDRJC Coaching Stock. *Journ. Irish Railway Record Soc.*, **14,** 129.
Half Yearly Reports of FVR, WDR and DR Companies, and of CDRJC up to the end of December 1912.
Annual Reports of CDRJC from 1913.
Annual Reports of S & L Railway Company from 1913.
Bradshaw's Railway Manual, Shareholders' Guide & Directory. Various editions.
Minutes of Board Meetings of FVR, WDR, DR, S & LR & Donegal Railway Station Companies, and of the CDRJC.
Working Timetables and Public Timetables of the various companies, and of the Joint Committee.
Appendices to the Working Timetable, CDRJC, editions of 1927, 1935, 1939 and 1950.
Private Papers of G. T. Glover.
Correspondence files and diagrams of the Loco. Department, GNR (I).
Tourist Programmes, CDRJC, editions of 1911, 1912, 1913, 1914 and 1915.
Board of Trade : Reports of Railway Accidents.

THE ILLUSTRATIONS

The author is grateful for permission to use photographs as follows :
The Belfast Telegraph, page 17 (above); Mr J. W. Blanchard, page 36 (above); the late Mr H. Fayle, pages 72 (below), 89 (above), 107 (above) and (below), 143 (above), 162 (below); Mr N. R. S. Foster, page 18 (above); Mr R. G. Jarvis, pages 54, 90 (above); Dr W. A. McCutcheon, page 161 (above); Dr I. S. Pearsall, page 36 (centre) and (below); Ulster Museum (Robert Welch Collection), page 126 (above); Valentine & Sons Ltd, Dundee, page 126 (below); the late Mr J. Macartney Robbins, page 184 (above); Mr P. B. Whitehouse, page 90 (below); the late Mr H. E. Wilson, MIMechE, MILocoE, page 71 (above).

Original builder's photographs formed the basis of pages 53, 108, 162 (above) and (centre).

Pages 17 (centre), 18 (centre) and (below), 35, 89 (centre) and (below), 107 (centre), 125, 143 (below), 144, 161 (below), 183, 184 (below), are from photographs by the author.

Publisher's Postscript

One of my most prized possessions is a ticket issued to my wife and me by the County Donegal Railways Joint Committee. It reads : 'PASS Mr. and Mrs. Thomas TO all stations FROM all stations AND BACK'. Alas, during a short tour of Ireland to study transport problems we had little time to take advantage of this magical document, and to my lasting regret I was unable to accept the offer of a footplate ride through the Barnesmore Gap.

We did, however, travel down the main line from Strabane to Killybegs and back, and it was during this journey that the idea of a book on the system was born. The railway immediately struck me, a dispassionate observer, as a remarkable enterprise. The first surprise, of course, was that there should be a narrow-gauge railway at all in so thinly-peopled an area as late as the mid-1950s. Merely to travel on the trains seemed to be stepping back in history. But any thoughts of the system being a mere quaint anachronism were rapidly dispelled. Until the end, the railway played a vital part in the life of the community it served, and it was run with exemplary efficiency.

Above all, the system impressed me with its friendliness. Here were none of the formalities and none of the dignity which so often seem designed to reduce the stature of passengers on standard-gauge railways. The County Donegal Railways were simple, domesticated —no impersonal organisation sheltering behind a mystique. Relations between staff and passengers, and among the staff themselves, were eminently human. Another attractive feature was the railway's unselfconsciousness; being so far removed from big centres it was relatively little visited by enthusiasts. There was no temptation to become a show or museum piece : the local population always came first.

Although my visit was short, I came away with many memories to cherish. Some of these centre on the enthusiastic welcome given me at the Stranorlar headquarters, with its loco and carriage shops, its sweet-stall in the booking hall, its diminutive footbridge and its incongruous clock-tower above the gentlemen's lavatory. The coaches stabled in the bay platform pending the departure of the next steam-hauled excursion were unlocked for examination, and the railcars were run out from the maintenance shed especially for me to photograph them. On departure, I sat beside the driver for the journey on to Killybegs. The grim grandeur of the Barnesmore Gap was impressive enough, but what most excited me was the last section, along the rough, tortuous and quite undeveloped Atlantic seaboard. The diesel horn echoed: the crossing keepers opened the gates; mothers and children rushed to the doorways of the whitewashed crossing cottages; and labourers digging tiny patches of peaty soil at the cliff's edge set their watches as we rollicked by. The driver apologised for the rough riding: I should have come when the track was as good as anything I would have seen in England, he said. Talking about England, 'My daddy once went there. I've never been myself, of course'. And so into the little port of Killybegs, where the most modern object was an oil tank wagon, a neat miniature of Esso's British wagons, standing in the siding.

Here was a service worth recording. An approach to the general manager, Mr B. L. Curran, who has provided much valuable help, resulted in an introduction to Dr Patterson. His work has given me great pleasure, as I am sure it will countless others. Its achievement lies not only in coming closely to grips with the history of the system itself, but in portraying it as a living part of Donegal life. That is how the railway will be remembered.

DAVID ST JOHN THOMAS

The above was written for the first edition of the book published in 1962. The second impression followed shortly. The book has now been substantially revised and extended. Alas, a new generation of railway lovers is growing up who never saw the County Donegal, but Dr Patterson's record will assure the unique system its fair place in history. The first edition, incidentally, set the pattern for the David & Charles *Railway History Series*, this edition being published almost simultaneously with the twenty-first title.

Index

Illustrations are indicated by bold type